Do *You* Know What's Invested in *You?*

*A Three-Part Biblical Teaching on the
Most Influential Factors in a Person's Life:
Self, Culture, and Purpose*

A READING GUIDE

PASTOR WILLIAM EVANS

Olympus Story House

Contents

Preface..v
Unit 1. Who You Are—A Study of "Self"...................................1
Introduction..1
Section 1: Secular Framework..2
Gaining understanding..2
Biological factors...3
Section 2: Spiritual Exposition..5
The spiritual body..5
Spiritual Truths..6
The four seeds..10
Seed one: curiosity..10
Seed two: faith...12
Seed three: steadfastness...14
Seed four: patience..15
Conclusion...17
Unit 1 Discussion Questions...18
Unit 2. Who You Are—A Study of "Culture"............................19
Introduction..19
Culture Defined..20
The Three Social Sciences..20
Avenues of Investigation...21
Nature versus Nurture...22
Cultural Subsets...24
Ideal versus Real Culture..26
Transition...28
The Firmament...29
The Waters and the Earth..31
Conclusion...32
Unit 2 Discussion Questions...34
Unit 3. Who You Are—A Study of "Purpose".............................35
Introduction..35
Purpose Defined...36
Socrates...36
Plato..37

Aristotle...38
Transition from Secular to Spiritual.................................39
Hints of Scripture in the Philosophy of Socrates............39
Hints of Scripture in the Philosophy of Plato...................43
Hints of Scripture in the Philosophy of Aristotle............45
Lessons to Remember as We Seek to Fulfill Our Purpose................45
Element one: social organization......................................46
Element two: customs and traditions.................................47
Element three: language...47
Element four: religion..48
Element five: form of government.....................................49
Bringing It All Together..50
Conclusion..51
Unit 3 Discussion Questions...67

PREFACE

I begin writing this preface with many thoughts in mind. Why did I write this book? As a believer in the Lord Jesus Christ, I struggled with identity issues. I have learned that the question of identity applies not only to the body of Christ but also to life in general. We are taught to find a model—"a system or thing used as an example to follow or imitate"—to fit in.

Early in life, as I struggled with my own identity, others whispered their ideas about who I was or who I would become. I sank into confusion. After giving my heart to the Lord Jesus Christ, God inspired me to look beyond the more superficial sources of identity and look to the eternal.

As I began this journey, I looked to my family and the Christian values they had instilled in me. I finally examined the culture and subculture in which I was reared. Up to then, I had accepted these as parts of who I was. I was accepting the beliefs of others as my own.

Yet an eternal yearning had a hold on me and would not release me. As I dug deeper, God asked me a question that he puts to all humanity every day: Do you know what's invested in you?

It is my belief that this book will serve as a guidepost pointing to our eternal selves. It is my hope that you will embrace this lesson as I have. If you do, you will learn not only who you truly are but also how you fit into this world and God's master plan.

May God enlighten you on this journey. Let us begin.

UNIT 1

Who You Are—A Study of "Self"

Introduction

Welcome, friends. It is an honor to speak with you today. I want to thank you for your presence as well as thank God for privileging me with the opportunity to embark upon this journey of spiritual awakening and awareness. This is a journey that will include a discussion of human origin. It is my sincere hope that it will assist you in finding a sense of identity and belonging, both in Christ and in the world. He has created for you, as well as revealed to you, just how important you are in His master plan.

As we begin this journey, I would like for you to think about this question: *Do you know what's invested in you?* There is much we will need to cover to answer this. We will begin by investigating three of the most influential factors in a person's life. These factors help a person define who they are and gain a deeper insight into not only where they come from but also where they are going and what they are meant to do in this existence. These three factors are *self, culture,* and *purpose.* These three factors play a vital role in grooming us into whom we are to become. If these are left unchecked, we could become something totally different. Therefore, we will address these issues as each build upon the previous one.

Let us begin with the most personal self. My objective is to give anyone embracing this lesson the knowledge to answer this fundamental question: *How do you define yourself as an individual?*

SECTION 1

Secular Framework

Gaining understanding

Many of us know that we are not born with knowledge of self. The idea of self was fashioned by our parents in the culture that we happened to be born into. This is done with good intentions, but ultimately, self-discovery lies with us. One way for people to gain a better understanding of who he or she is as an individual is to investigate the roots of his/her family. *Genealogy,* the study of an individual's family history, is a useful tool when a person is seeking to learn more about their background, such as who their ancestors were, where they came from, where they established their foundations, and the like. Although this is certainly part of the overall picture, a person should not stop there; doing so gives a narrow view of who you truly are. Each of us is unique, and even though a person's family does indeed contribute a great deal to their identity and personality, there is much more that defines that person's makeup. An individual should also look to the biological factors—the study of life and living organisms. Doing so will allow a person to gain a systematic understanding of the origin of all humanity.

This is important because it causes us to abandon a tribal view of self and helps us to embrace and become more open to our commonalities. For example, we see this in small children as they are more open to play well with others because they do not focus on differences; they focus on commonalities, and this helps them become more well-rounded and empathetic. Let us not be naive. As we grow, we know that there are cultural views and experiences that change this perspective; however, we are still left with the choice to adhere to what is right.

Science, absent of spirituality, can only give a one-sided view of this or any issue. When coupled with spiritual truth, however, such a field of study can be greatly beneficial. Not only does it allow us to analyze the genetic makeup of everyone but also the uniformity of the human body despite any perceived dissimilarities. These differences can be economic, gender based, ethnic, cultural, and so on. Science simultaneously allows us to gain a specialized view of our own genetic makeup, as well as a broader view of humanity at large, never allowing us to forget that, ultimately, we are all members of the same race of creature—human beings given life by our Creator. This leads us to a twofold question: *As human beings, in what ways are we similar? In what ways are we different?*

Biological factors

The investigation of self—when we take the time to study biology, we will learn that the human body is structurally organized into three levels. First, there are *cells.* Cells are individual entities, each of which has a specific task to accomplish to sustain life. For example, one cell may assist in digesting food, while another may assist in carrying messages to and from the brain, and yet another in the fighting of diseases that enter the body. Second, we have tissues, which are a family of cells that live very closely together and work together to accomplish the same tasks, for example, the epithelial tissue, which consists of specialized cells that cover the exterior of the body like the skin and the internal of the body like blood vessels and intestine. Third, there is the *nervous system,* which senses what is going on around us and then responds in an appropriate way, for example, regulating the heart rate to flexing the hand or foot.

Cells and tissues come together to form organs, which are relatively independent parts of the body that carry out one or more special functions. Examples of organs include the eyes, ears, heart, lungs, and liver. These organs work together to form an organ system. An organ system is not just any collection of organs but a collection of organs that are arranged a certain way to perform a certain function. The most obvious example of an organ system is the heart and the surrounding circulatory system. The circulatory system functions primarily to circulate blood to the various parts of the body. The primary components of the circulatory system are the heart, blood, and blood vessels such as arteries, veins, and capillaries. There are eleven major organ systems in the human body, and each one is essential for life to be sustained.

This is true for all humanity.

SECTION 2

Spiritual Exposition

The spiritual body

A t this point, you may be wondering why I would take time to share this information. You may be questioning if it really has any spiritual value. Though it may surprise you, the answer to this question is yes. All the information I have just shared forms the basis of the model Apostle Paul used in *1 Corinthians 12:12 (King James Version)* to illustrate interdependence and unity within the church: "For as the body is one, and has many members, and all the members of that one body, being many, are one body: so also is Christ."

Paul's decision to use the human body to illustrate this was not by chance. His message was Spirit led. God designed the human body as He did, and inspired Paul to speak the words he did, because this model is a perfect example of how a family, a church, or a business should work. Yes, each part of the body—both literally in a biological sense and spiritually in an eternal sense—exists as its own unit. Each part also cooperates to form a single entity; each one depends upon the others, either directly or indirectly, to function normally. This is not exclusive to a certain group of people. Rather, this is true for humanity and the universal family of God.

You see, whether you were born into poverty or riches, whether you are male or female, and whether you are black, white, or brown, none of these matter. What matters is remembering you are indeed a unique creation of God, imbued with your own strengths, abilities, gifts, and purpose. As well, an integral part of something much larger—a body of brothers and sisters bound by our physical and spiritual makeup the world over. The health of that body—in fact, its very existence—is dependent upon how you function both alone and in conjunction with those around you. This leads to a third fundamental question: *What do you think it means that we have been born in the image and likeness of God?*

Spiritual Truths

There is obviously much more to the science of biology than the simple elements previously noted. For now, this brief introduction will serve our purpose. Remember, science alone cannot provide us with an adequate understanding of eternal topics. As I touched upon just a moment ago, without a spiritual context and connection, such information is ultimately meaningless. For a broader view of personal identity and belonging, we must look to the Word of God and allow His Spirit to reveal to us the truths surrounding the origin of humanity.

In *Genesis 2:7,* scripture states, "And the LORD God formed man *of* the dust of the ground and breathed into his nostrils the breath of life; and man became a living soul."

This passage deals with three components: First, we have the "dust of the ground." Dust is defined as fine particles of matter. What is matter? Matter is the substance of which all material is made. Matter can be directly experienced through the senses. It has properties that can be measured, such as mass, volume, and density, and qualitative properties, such as taste, smell, and color. All physical bodies in the universe are made of matter: galaxies, stars, and planets, rocks, water, and air. Living organisms like plants, animals, and humans are also composed of matter. For example, the water we drink, the food we eat, and everything we see are made of matter. When the structure and composition of matter is investigated, it breaks matter into smaller and smaller pieces.

As stated earlier in the lesson, living organisms are made up of cells. Cells are composed of molecules, which are sets of atoms bonded together. Our body is our outer part containing our five senses with which we contact all the things of the physical, material realm. This is what gives us our connection to the physical world we inhabit.

Second, the passage talks about the breath of life, and this leads us to a different view of biology. I would like to introduce the term *heredity,* which is the passing on of traits from parents to their offspring, either through asexual reproduction or sexual reproduction; this is where the offspring, cells, or organisms acquire the genetic information of their parents. Every child inherits genes from both of their biological parents, and these genes in turn express specific traits. Some of these traits may be physical, such as hair, eye, and skin color. On the other hand, some genes may also carry the risk of certain diseases and disorders that parents may pass on to their offspring.

Why is this relevant? Just as our physical being represents the genetics of our earthly parents, the breath of life gives us the genetics of our Heavenly Father. Recall from *Genesis 2:7* that the human spirit originated from God as His "breath of life." And according to *Genesis 1:26a,* it states, "And God said; Let us make man in our image, after our likeness."

This gene powers our bodies so that we can function as spiritual beings. Our spirit is our innermost part with which we contact God and substantiate all the things of the spiritual realm. The spirit in man gives us the abilities that make us human in the image of God. We have self-awareness, intellect, creativity, and the ability to appreciate beauty. We also possess a unique personality and temperament and the capabilities to manifest the attributes of our Heavenly Father.

Just as we are connected to the physical world and must learn about our physical self, we are created as spiritual beings and must learn about our spiritual self. This is clearly explained in *1 Corinthians 2:11–14* where it states,

> For what man knoweth the things of a man, save the spirit of man which is in him? Even so the things of God knoweth no man, but the Spirit of God. Now we have received, not the spirit of the world, but the spirit which is of God, that we might know the things that are freely given to us of God. Which things also we speak, not in the words which man's wisdom teacheth, but which the Holy Ghost teacheth, comparing spiritual things with spiritual. But the natural man receiveth not the things of the Spirit of God: for they are foolishness unto him: neither can he know them, because they are spiritually discerned.

Jesus addresses this in *John 3:6* where it states, "That which is born of the flesh is flesh; and that which is born of the Spirit is spirit."

In this passage, Jesus specifies a clear distinction between that which is born of the flesh and of the spirit. The Bible is consistent in this distinction.

In this overview of the natural and spiritual creation of humanity, we are given a glimpse of only the duality of humanity. However, humanity at this point is still not whole.

This leads to the third component of the soul. The word soul in the Bible is a translation of the Hebrew word *nephesh* and the Greek word *psyche*. The Hebrew word literally means "a creature that breathes," and the Greek word means "a living being." The soul is the entire creature, not something inside that survives the death of the body. Consider how the Bible shows that the human soul is the whole person: When God created the first man, Adam, the Bible says that "man became a living soul. Adam was not *given* a soul—he *became* a *living* soul, or person."

The divine essence of the human soul is what sets the human being above and apart from all other creations, even the angels. The angel may be more spiritual, but the human being is godlier. No creation can possess true freedom of choice—a creation, by definition, has and consists of only what its Creator has imparted to it; this is its "nature," and its every inclination and action will be dictated by that nature. It is only in the human soul that the Creator imparted His own essence. The human soul is thus the only truly "supranatural" being (aside from the Creator)—a being that is not limited by its own nature, a being that can transcend itself, a being that can choose to not merely react to its environment but to act upon it, and a being whose choices and actions are therefore of true *significance.*

The soul is provided with a compass and guidebook to navigate the challenge of physical life and the resources to fortify it. The Word of God is the divine "blueprint for creation" that guides and instructs the soul on its mission. The Word of God is also "food for the soul": By studying the Word, the soul ingests and digests the divine wisdom and is supplied with the divine energy to persevere in its mission and overcome its challenges.

The soul, the "person" of man, is likewise composed of three parts: the mind, the will, and the emotion. God's Word proves this clearly.

First, the scriptures consistently identify the mind as part of the soul, for example, in *Psalm 139:14:* "I will praise thee; for I am fearfully and wonderfully made: marvellous are thy works; and that my soul knoweth right well." Knowledge, no doubt, pertains to the mind. This is evident in *Lamentations 3:19–20:* "Remembering mine affliction and my misery, the wormwood and the gall. My soul hath them still in remembrance, and is humbled in me." These verses clearly indicate that there is a part of the soul that knows and remembers; this part is the mind.

8

Then there is the will, which is also part of the soul. An example can be found in Joshua 24:15: "And if it seem evil unto you to serve the Lord, choose you this day whom ye will serve; whether the gods which your fathers served that were on the other side of the flood, or the gods of the Amorites, in whose land ye dwell: but as for me and my house, we will serve the Lord." Then there is Deuteronomy 30:19–20: "I call heaven and earth to record this day against you, that I have set before you life and death, blessing and cursing: therefore choose life, that both thou and thy seed may live."

Finally, we can see from the Word that the emotions are part of the soul.

> Tell me, O thou whom my soul loveth, where thou feedest, where thou makest thy flock to rest at noon: for why should I be as one that turneth aside by the flocks of thy companions? (Song of Solomon 1:7 KJV)

> And, behold, a certain lawyer stood up, and tempted him, saying, "Master, what shall I do to inherit eternal life?" He said unto him, "What is written in the law? How readest thou?" And he answering said, "Thou shalt love the Lord thy God with all thy heart, and with all thy soul, and with all thy strength, and with all thy mind; and thy neighbour as thyself." And he said unto him, "Thou hast answered right: this do, and thou shalt live." (Luke 10:25–28)

There is more to the souls of humans. By nature, we are creatures of desires and longings, living beings who eagerly seek to live but are unable to acquire or preserve life by ourselves. The *soul* refers to the whole person in need of God, who is the only one who can preserve a human being or extinguish the self forever. This is evident in *Matthew 10:28:* "And fear not them which kill the body, but are not able to kill the soul: but rather fear him which is able to destroy both soul and body in hell."

Therefore, *nephesh/psyche* refers to the totality of the person as a center of life, emotions, feelings, and longings that can be fully realized only in union with God.

To review, our body is our outer part containing our five senses with which we contact all the things of the physical and material realm. Our soul is our inner part containing our mind, emotion, and will with which we contact all the things of the psychological realm. Our spirit is our innermost part with which we contact God and substantiate all the things of the spiritual realm.

My dear brothers and sisters, we see in Genesis 2:7 that God created humanity whole with each component working together to glorify Him on the earth.

The four seeds

Seed one: curiosity

Dear brothers and sisters, as we navigate our way through this journey of spiritual self-discovery, I would like to remind you that this journey is to raise our awareness about who we are and for each of us to ask ourselves, "Do you know what's invested in you?" As we move forward in this endeavor, let the following four seeds work in combination with the Spirit of God to guide you.

As we move forward to give insight into these four seeds, I would like you to answer this fundamental question: *Which of the four seeds currently plays the most important role in your life?*

The first seed is that of curiosity, the strong desire to know or learn about something. We demonstrate our curiosity about the world around us daily. Some believe we are driven in this regard due to an internal hunger or thirst to know more. This belief, called the *drive theory,* views curiosity as a naturally occurring urge that must be satisfied in much the same way that we satisfy our hunger by eating. Another belief, the *incongruity theory,* maintains that our curiosity is motivated when we are presented with something that does not fit into our normal understanding of the world. We have been taught to view the universe as predictable and orderly. When this is challenged, our curiosity is piqued.

Those who hold to the drive theory believe that curiosity is simply another trait that human beings possess, while those who hold to the incongruity theory believe that external situations evoke it. If we look to Scripture, specifically *Genesis 2:16–17,* it would appear that the latter view is the one which rings true: "And the LORD God commanded the man, saying, of every tree of the garden you may freely eat: But of the tree of the knowledge of good and evil, you shall not eat of it: for in the day that you eat thereof you will surely die."

Note that Adam's curiosity was not aroused by this statement from God. There was no internal drive urging him to test the validity of what he had been told. Rather, he simply accepted what God said as truth.

Curiosity was not challenged until *Genesis 3:1–6:*

> Now the serpent was more subtle than any beast of the field which the Lord God had made. And he said unto the woman, yea, has God said, ye shall not eat of every tree of the garden? And the woman said unto the serpent, we may eat of the fruit of the trees of the garden: But of the fruit of the tree which is in the middle of the garden, God has said you shall not eat of it; neither shall you touch it, lest you die. And the serpent said unto the woman, you shall not surely die: For God does know that in the day you eat thereof, then your eyes shall be opened, and you shall be as gods, knowing good and evil. And when the woman saw that the tree *was* good for food, and that it *was* pleasant to the eyes, and a tree to be desired to make *one* wise, she took of the fruit thereof, and did eat, and gave also unto her husband with her; and he did eat.

When a direct challenge was posed to what Adam and Eve had previously accepted without question, their curiosity was awakened. We know that in verses 7 through 11 that this action caused immediate spiritual death, and humanity was introduced to a fallen state; where there was once union, there is division. When the command was violated, this action caused a ripple effect throughout creation because as Apostle Paul wrote in *Romans 5:12,* "Wherefore, as by one man sin entered into the world, and death by sin; and so death passed upon all men, for that all have sinned."

No more was there harmony because humanity was not whole. This passage would seem to give grim hope, but the apostle comes back in *Romans 5:19:* "For as by one man's disobedience many were made sinners, so by the obedience of one shall many be made righteous."

Another scriptural example relevant to this topic can be found in *Exodus 3:1–3:*

Now Moses kept the flock of Jethro, his father in law, the priest of Midian: and he led the flock to the backside of the desert, and came to the mountain of God, *even* to Horeb. And the angel of the Lord appeared unto him in a flame of fire out of the midst of a bush: and he looked, and, behold, the bush burned with fire, and the bush was not consumed. And Moses said, I will now turn aside, and see this great sight, why the bush is not burnt.

Again, it was the abnormal—something beyond the ordinary— for these biblical figures that motivated them to be curious. This would suggest that human beings are motivated to question their environment and circumstances when faced with incongruence rather than simply an inner urge.

This, of course, may be a matter of debate. What is far from debatable, however, is that these two scriptural examples demonstrate how curiosity can either mislead us into wrongdoing or propel us to greater understanding. I urge you, in your own lives, to allow it to do the latter for curiosity—in its purest and most innocent form—leads us to *discovery.* This is very important in this lesson because curiosity will help uncover something previously unknown, such as our true self, including *knowledge,* a familiarity with self that is gained through experience or education, and purpose, the reason for which you were created or exist.

Seed two: faith

The second seed is that of faith, complete trust, or confidence in someone or something. It is generally understood that there are two types of faith, natural and spiritual. The former has its origin in the physical realm and is supported by a person's natural physical senses and experiences. This type of faith is based on what can be seen with the one's eyes and felt with one's hands—the familiarity involved in sitting on a chair and trusting it to support your weight. The latter has its origin in the spiritual realm. As defined by Scripture in *Hebrews 11:1,* "Now faith is the substance of things hoped for, the evidence of things not seen." Perhaps a bit more in-depth means of defining faith can be found in the words of the same verse in the Amplified Bible: "the assurance (the confirmation, the title deed) of the things [we] hope for, being the proof of things [we] do not see and the conviction of their reality."

What this means is that spiritual faith operates on what our inner being perceives as truth rather than what is revealed as such by our senses. Capable of either waning or growing, this type of faith is a spiritual substance that operates from within. Chapter 11 in the book of Hebrews is devoted to extolling this type of faith in person after person throughout biblical history. Naturally, it is this type of faith that I urge you to cultivate.

Do not, for one moment, doubt that you can for faith is a gift that has been given to all humanity.

> For I say, through the grace given unto me, to every man that is among you, not to think of *himself* more highly than he ought to think; but to think soberly, according as God has dealt to every man the measure of faith. Every human being can believe; what we believe is based upon what we hear. (Romans 12:3)

> Faith comes by hearing, and hearing by the Word of God. (Romans 10:17)

God speaks belief into us through the power of His Word. He tells us who we are, what we can do, and how we can accomplish His will. This faith must be developed over time.

> And the apostles said unto the Lord, Increase our faith. And the Lord said, If you had faith as a grain of mustard seed, you might say unto this sycamore tree, be you plucked up by the root, and be you planted in the sea; and it should obey you. (Luke 17:5–6)

Here the Lord Jesus gives an important message regarding the development of one's spiritual faith. It must be put into action every bit as much as the natural faith a person displays when they sit in a chair believing it will support their weight. As we do this, as we seek to live lives defined by true spiritual faith, it leads to *confidence,* certainty about the truth of who God is and who we are in His will, as well as to *obedience,* compliance with the requests God makes of us and directions God gives us, both of which are vital in order to be submissive to God's will.

Seed three: steadfastness

The third seed is the seed of *steadfastness.* Scripture abounds with examples of individuals who exhibited this characteristic, but aside from the Lord Jesus Christ, perhaps none did so more notably than Job. In *Job 1:1–22,* you will find this man of the land of Uz. The scripture says that he was perfect and upright and one that feared God and eschewed evil.

He had ten children, seven sons, and three daughters. He was very rich with substance, seven thousand sheep, three thousand camels, five hundred yoke of oxen, and five hundred she donkeys. The scripture describes him as the greatest man of the East.

The scripture tells us that all of this would come under attack with the purpose of trying to prove that Job's integrity was predicated based on the things he possessed.

In reading these scriptures, you find that the attack on Job centers on the things he has. This tells us that Satan was trying to prove that everything Job had was his reason for holding on to his integrity.

All of this was done by Satan to prove to God that no one would truly be dedicated to Him without the blessing of the things He gives them. Satan believed that if all was taken away, Job would curse God to His face. This was true then and is still true today. Like Job, we must look to God as our source and trust that God always has our best interest in mind.

This passage concludes by saying, "Then Job arose, and rent his mantle, and shaved his head, and fell down upon the ground, and worshipped, and said, Naked came I out of my mother's womb, and naked shall I return thither: the LORD gave, and the Lord has taken away; blessed be the name of the LORD. In all this Job sinned not, nor charged God foolishly."

Many times, when one is under attack, the person tends to respond with rebellion, becoming bitter and begin to blame God for the difficulties that have arisen. This passage, however, shows us how to properly respond to the strategic attacks that Satan may bring against us. Rebellion is the enemy of steadfastness. What every one of us must learn is how to deny the emotional influences in our lives. We must instead continue moving forward to execute our purposes without losing sight of them. Emotions are God-given, but emotional responses to external circumstances and situations are often inconsistent with the Word of God. Without surrender to and guidance by the Spirit, it becomes easy for a person to fall victim to Satan's attempts to sway them away from God's plan or message.

A person must therefore be persistent in adhering to the Word of God and the faith God has instilled within them as Apostle Paul extols the church of Corinth in *1 Corinthians 15:58:* "Therefore, my beloved brethren, be you steadfast, unmovable, always abounding in the work of the Lord, forasmuch as you know that your labor is not in vain in the Lord." To do otherwise is to allow circumstances to define us as we give them power to direct our course. When a person instead remains steadfast and adopts this trait into their character, it leads to *consistency,* reliability, stability in one's convictions, and *trustworthiness,* both in the eyes of others and in the eyes of God.

Seed four: patience

The final seed is the seed of *patience,* a seed that grants a person the ability to wait for the fruition of something. Job again serves as an excellent example of someone who adopted this trait into his character:

> Again there was a day when the sons of God came to present themselves before the LORD, and Satan came also among them to present himself before the Lord. And the Lord said unto Satan, "From whence come you?" And Satan answered the Lord, and said, "From going to and fro in the earth, and from walking up and down in it." And the Lord said unto Satan, "Have you considered my servant Job, that *there* is none like him in the earth, a perfect and an upright man, one that fears God, and eschews evil? and still he holds fast his integrity, although you moved me against him, to destroy him without cause." And Satan answered the Lord, and said, "Skin for skin, yea, all that a man has will he give for his life. But put forth Your hand now, and touch his bone and his flesh, and he will curse You to Your face." And the Lord said unto Satan, "Behold, he *is* in your hand; but save his life." So went Satan forth from the presence of the Lord, and smote Job with sore boils from the sole of his foot unto his crown. And he took him a potsherd to scrape himself withal; and he sat down among the ashes. Then said his wife unto him, "Do you still retain your integrity? Curse God, and

die." But he said unto her, "you speak as one of the foolish women speaks. What? Shall we receive good at the hand of God, and shall we not receive evil? In all this did not Job sin with his lips?" (Job 2:1–10)

The forces of evil can be aggressive in their attacks. Many of us have had some experiences with these attacks. I remember going out to witness downtown Dallas under the freeway as I was talking to some homeless people there. This guy caught my attention because he was very articulate. My first thought was, Why are you here? Yes, I must admit that drugs, alcoholism, etc., cross my mind. As we began to talk, the conversation began to get comfortable, where we both started dropping our guard. At this moment, I felt comfortable enough to ask, How did you end up under the freeway? His eyes welled up, and he told about the type of money he was making, how well he lived, the home, and the car, but the most important thing was his family and how much he loved them. While at work one day, he gets a call. His family is in a wreck, and they were killed. He said it shook him to his core, and at that point, he was lost. That was how he ended up under the freeway. What could I say at that point? I could not change what happened, but I could point to the one that could restore that which was lost, but he had to understand that it would begin with him. This encounter wasn't just for him. It was for me also because I realized that all I have seen was the state of the person, but God taught me to pay attention to the journey because we never know what is the reasoning for why people do, say, or end up where they are. This passage teaches us that we can overcome all obstacles if only we wait and rely upon the Lord. Despite all that happened to Job, he held on and maintained his integrity. In the end, all that he lost was restored because he never wavered in his belief that all things happen for purpose. In time, he knew that purpose would be fulfilled, even if he never came to know what all the attacks meant.

In Romans 8:28, it says, "All things work together for good to them that love God, to them who are called according to His purpose." This verse also teaches that one must accept delay or disappointment not with frustration but with understanding, knowing that God's delays are not God's denials. When this is understood, it becomes far easier for a person to recognize that being patient doesn't mean sitting around waiting for things to happen. Rather, working as hard and as long as is necessary, without giving up, until he or she reaches his or her destination. The cultivation of patience in this manner leads to experience as an individual personally encounters, undergoes, or lives through a period of trial or delayed expectation. It also leads to growth, the process of gradual increase and maturity, a psychological term used to indicate how a person responds to his or her environment or circumstances in an appropriate and adaptive manner.

CONCLUSION

This, my brothers and sisters, draws us near the end of this first step in our ongoing journey. Before I close, let me first encourage you to understand and remember that the illustration of the human body as used by Apostle Paul to represent the church is not a new one. From the beginning of eternity, God always intended for the design He used for our bodies to be a literal symbol of the spiritual design of His church. The sacrifice that Jesus made for us was not for naught. It was made so humanity would have the choice between a sinful state and a redemptive state.

What is hid in the sinful state is the origins of humanity found in *Genesis 1:26–27* that tells us that humanity was made in God's image, after His *likeness,* and was given *dominion* over everything on earth. What is revealed in the redemptive state is that we have God's DNA in us; this is evident in *1 John 4:4:* "You are of God, little children, and have overcome them: because greater is He that is in you, than he that is in the world."

I asked you a question very early on in this message. I pose that question to you again now: *Do you know what's invested in you?* If you do not know, are you willing to nurture *curiosity* to uncover what Scripture says about this even if the revelations are sometimes difficult to hear? Are you willing to accept, through *faith,* the truths Scripture sets forth even if they contradict what you have been taught to believe? Are you willing to remain *steadfast* in the face of trials even though "in whom the god of this world hath blinded the minds of them which believe not, will do everything in his power to keep you in his embrace" (2 Corinthians 4:4a)? Are you willing to demonstrate *patience* even though this journey will require time, effort, and energy to complete?

If your answer is no, my brothers and sisters, the first step is to follow the blueprint laid out in *Romans 10:9–10:* "That if thou shalt confess with thy mouth the Lord Jesus, and shalt believe in thine heart that God hath raised him from the dead, thou shalt be saved.

17

For with the heart man believeth unto righteousness; and with the mouth confession is made unto salvation." I encourage you to humble yourself and allow the power of God through the Holy Spirit to draw you through God's agape love. Agape is an unconditional love that looks beyond your faults and sees your need.

If you have already done this, I encourage you to continue developing the four seeds outlined in this lesson. I invite you all to join me again as we move on to the next lesson and delve more deeply into this issue, discussing our state as related to culture and how it influences us.

Until next time. Remember you are more than what your society or your circumstances say you are. You are a creature fashioned and blessed by the highest god, sincerely and deeply loved. So as you embrace this lesson, think like it, talk like it, and live like it, and in doing so, you will become an example to those around you, evidence that this life can be lived.

May the Lord bless and keep you all in His glorious light and love. Amen.

Unit 1 Discussion Questions

1. How do you define yourself as an individual?
2. What are the key factors or traits you use in outlining who you are?
3. In what ways are we, as human beings, similar?
4. In what ways are we different?
5. What does it mean that—despite any differences—God desires all of us to become members of the body of Christ?
6. What do you think it means that we have been born in the image and likeness of God?
7. What impact does such a divine heritage have upon human existence?
8. What responsibilities does such a heritage impart to us and, more specifically, to you personally?
9. Which of the four seeds currently plays the most important role in your life? (Please note that you can identify more than one.)
10. How can this seed both assist and prevent you in continuing your journey of spiritual self-discovery?

UNIT 2

Who You Are—A Study of "Culture"

Introduction

Welcome, dear brothers and sisters. Again, it is a great honor to be blessed with the opportunity to speak to you. As always, I want to thank God for granting us this time together. After all, without Him, none of us would be here. Let us not take this opportunity for granted. Instead, let us use it to honor and glorify Him by studying His Word and applying it to our lives.

In the previous lesson, do you know what's invested in you? We investigated one of the three most influential factors in a person's life—self. Through our discussion of the science of biology, we gained a systematic understanding of the origin of all humanity. Through our discussion of the Word of God, we learned that we are more than simply warm bodies but rather living beings imbued with strengths, abilities, gifts, and—above all—purpose. In addition, we also introduced the four seeds with which all humanity is invested—curiosity, faith, steadfastness, and patience—as well as examined how these seeds should take root in our lives if we are to reap the fullness of what the Lord truly has planned for us. All of this was done to give insight to a fundamental question.

Let us now move on to the second of these three factors—*culture*—which will give us a different perspective and a broader view of the subject of "Do you know what's invested in you?" as we continue to glean what the Spirit would next have us learn from our studies.

How would you describe the culture to which you belong?

Culture Defined

To begin, we must first gain an understanding of what this term means. Simply put, culture consists of the beliefs, behaviors, objects, and other characteristics common to members of a group or society. Culture encompasses language, religion, cuisine, social habits, music, and arts. It is transmitted from one generation to the next by communication and imitation, often subconsciously and without a second thought.

Culture is closely linked to the concept of identity. Identity is who you are, the way you think about yourself, the way you are viewed by the world, and the characteristics that define you. We see this when we observe people that share a culture; they feel a sense of belonging. However, even though these differences are noticeable and sometimes exploited because we consider our culture to be superior, as believers in the god who has created all humanity, we must actively work to avoid this limited view. If we examine any culture closely, we will see many similarities that make us more alike than different. One means of doing this comes by looking at culture through various prisms of social science, namely, those of archaeology, anthropology, and sociology.

Why are social sciences so important?

The Three Social Sciences

The first of these scientific fields, *archaeology,* is the scientific study of material remains (such as tools, pottery, jewelry, stone walls, and monuments) of past human life and activities. These are the remains of the culture of a people. We often take this work for granted. Without archaeology, we wouldn't have evidence of human prehistory and history, from the development of the first stone tools in East Africa 3.3 million years ago up until recent decades. We wouldn't be able to learn from historical societies and their distinct ethnic and cultural groupings according to their material culture. So when you have time, go to the museum in your city, and appreciate the work that these archaeologists are doing.

The second of these scientific fields is *anthropology,* the science that deals with the origins, physical and cultural development, biological characteristics, and social customs and beliefs of humankind. Anthropology is the systematic study of humanity, with the goal of understanding our evolutionary origins, our distinctiveness as a species, and the great diversity in our forms of social existence across the world and through time. Anthropology seeks to uncover principles of behavior that apply to all human communities. To an anthropologist, diversity itself—seen in body shapes and sizes, customs, clothing, speech, religion, and worldview—provides a frame of reference for understanding any single aspect of life in any given community.

Sociology's purpose is to understand how human actions and consciousness both shape and are shaped by surrounding cultural and social structures. This field studies, analyzes, and explains important matters in our personal lives, our communities, and the world. At the personal level, sociology investigates the social causes and consequences of such things as romantic love, racial and gender identity, family conflict, deviant behavior, aging, and religious faith. At the societal level, sociology examines and explains matters like crime and law, poverty and wealth, prejudice and discrimination, schools and education, business firms, urban community, and social movements. At the global level, sociology studies such phenomena as population growth and migration, war and peace, and economic development. Sociologists emphasize the careful gathering and analysis of evidence about social life to develop and enrich our understanding of key social processes. The research methods and theories of sociology yield powerful insights into the social processes shaping human lives and social problems and prospects in the contemporary world. The better we understand those social processes, the more clearly we recognize those forces shaping our personal experiences and the outcomes of our own lives.

Avenues of Investigation

There are many different avenues social scientists in these fields can pursue. Some may analyze physical *artifacts,* objects made by a human being, such as an item of cultural or historical interest.

Examples of cultural artifacts include almost anything—from pots and books to religious items, clothing, and tools or gadgets. A cultural artifact is any artifact or item that sheds light on the way a society lived, thought, or otherwise expressed itself. There are many examples of artifacts in museums all over the world. All cultures have artifacts that represent core beliefs and customs.

Others may study the *celebrations, ceremonies,* and *rituals* of a people. These factors represent the established processes or practices that are repeated in specific circumstances and hold specific meanings. For example, a birthday is an occasion when a person celebrates the anniversary of their first day of life. Birthdays are rites of passage celebrated in numerous cultures and often include gifts and parties. Many religions celebrate the birth of their founders with special holidays like Christmas.

The culture of a group is often also transmitted through the *stories, myths,* and *legends* they share. Interestingly, regardless of the group from whom they originate, there is an underlying uniformity when it comes to elements of these accounts. For example, in virtually every culture, narratives include a hero, often a representation of the prototypical member of the society in question, as well as a villain, occasionally unnamed but always shady and untrustworthy. The stories that center on these figures evolve in a classic format with the villain ultimately being overtaken and vanquished by the hero and the innocent being rescued. Thrown into the bargain is an overarching lesson on the greatness of the culture from which these stories develop. Even our modern American culture follows this outline as this is the plot in most of our books, television shows, and movies. Regardless of the society from which they come, the power of these stories resides in what, when, and how they are told and also the effect they have on those who hear, read, or view them.

One final influence we should discuss involves *symbols* and *symbolic actions.* Symbols are objects that stand for or trigger ideas, images, or beliefs in the minds of those to whom they are significant. They remind members of a certain culture of the rules upon which their society has been founded and, thereby, act as a type of shorthand that keeps people aligned. Flags are an extremely easy way to identify a culture. The colors and emblems chosen by each culture for its flag are deeply symbolic.

If we hope to effectively interact with people from different cultures and backgrounds, we must be consciously aware of the cultural elements like economics, geography, history, politics, and religion and how they can influence intercultural interactions and relationships.

What are your innate characteristics as compared to your experiences?

Nature versus Nurture

With the time and attention, we have devoted to gaining an understanding of the previously mentioned factors that may influence a culture. It is appropriate that we now also explore a concept known as the *nature versus nurture theory*. This theory weighs the relative importance of an individual's innate characteristics as compared to their experiences.

As you may have guessed, nature refers to the biological factors that contribute to the genetic makeup we inherit from our ancestors, the inherited attributes that influence our development. Some of these attributes appear in virtually everyone. For instance, almost every human being has the potential to learn to walk, to understand language, to imitate others, to use simple tools, and to draw inferences about how other people view the world. These are universal human genes. It should be noted that inherited characteristics and tendencies are not always evident at birth. Many physical features emerge gradually during the maturation process. Other genes create immediate differences. A person's stature, eye color, and skin pigmentation, for example, are also largely determined by genes.

Nurture refers to the environmental conditions that influence the growth process. Our experiences throughout the various conditions we may encounter affect all aspects of our development. A person matures physically through the nutrition he or she gains, the activity he or she is involved in, and the stress he or she successfully manages or avoids. Intellectually, a person matures through informal experiences and formal instruction. A person also matures socially through interactions and relationships with peers and adult role models. With positive environmental support, a person can thrive, but as we are aware, environmental conditions are not always nurturing. Some people, for example, grow up in homes with abusive family members and must look beyond them for stable, affectionate care. Although it is not impossible, it is much more difficult to flourish under such circumstances.

Historically, many theorists have considered nature and nurture to be separate and rival influences. Some have stated that biological factors are ultimately responsible for growth, while others have maintained that it is our environment that shapes us. In the more modern era, developmental theorists have come to realize that nature and nurture intermesh in our lives, and thus, both play a role in human development. The truth of the matter is that nature and nurture each exert an individual and equally influencing sway on human development and, by extension, on human societies.

What do you contribute to the subset?

Cultural Subsets

Everything we have discussed to this point works to define the culture of a society and the subsets that develop from it. These *subcultures* are unique ways of life shared by smaller groups of people who also belong to the larger culture system.

One culture often contains many subcultures, each with distinct norms and customs that separate them from the broader culture by which they are enveloped. An individual can be a part of several subcultures simultaneously.

In every country, there is evidence of this; from the northern, southern, eastern, and western part of the country, the cultures are different, and even inside these different regions, there are differences.

High culture is an example of one such subculture. This term refers to the subculture shared by the elite members of a society. Many people mistakenly associate the word *culture* with high culture, suggesting that *cultured* individuals are those who attend the ballet, collect museum-quality artwork, and dine at expensive restaurants. It is important to note that sociologists do not consider high culture to be better than any other subculture but merely different. This difference is in behavior. Those that are a part of the elite of a society don't tend to dine at a McDonald's. They eat at expensive restaurants like the Mansion on Turtle Creek that serve exquisite cuisine, serve imported wine, and play classical music.

There is also *popular culture,* which is the dominant subculture shared by most of a society's population. The elements of this subculture are music, art, literature, fashion, and television. These have mass accessibility and appeal. These elements are accumulated and enjoyed primarily by members of non-elite groups such as the working, middle, and lower classes. In their communities, McDonald's is accessible and cost-efficient.

Woven also into subcultures are people who migrate from their native countries to take up residence in new regions, bringing the elements of their native cultures with them. Because this is true, the population of any given country can be quite diverse as no country consists entirely of any single culture. Multiculturalism is a situation in which all the different cultural or racial groups in a society have equal rights and opportunities, and none is ignored or regarded as unimportant. The preservation of different cultural identities within a unified society is very significant. Multiculturalism is the belief that cultural differences should be respected and celebrated rather than ridiculed and segregated.

Does your culture relate more to the ideal or real culture and how?

Ideal versus Real Culture

There is one final topic we must discuss before we begin to investigate how all of this relates to Scripture—the discrepancy that exists between a society's *real culture,* the values and norms members of a society adhere to, and its *ideal culture,* the values and norms said members claim to have.

Real culture reflects an adaptable value system established upon guidelines for preferred behavior; the concepts of right and wrong are differentiated, but what is deemed acceptable is relative rather than absolute. In stark contrast, ideal culture represents a glorified, uncompromising value system that outlines perfect conduct. When it is used as a standard, behavior can be judged as either right or wrong; neither gray areas nor any exceptions exist.

Can the ideal culture truly be apprehended? Explain how.

Transition from Secular to Spiritual

At this point, you may be wondering about all the things that influence you as you grow in your own culture, but we will narrow the scope of influence. We transition now into our exploration of what the Word of God says about the *truly* ideal culture and how it influences everyone in every culture.

The Bible consists of sixty-six books. It was composed by many different writers—both Jews and Gentiles alike—of almost every social rank, from uneducated peasants, herdsmen, and fishermen to learned statesmen, priests, and kings. Most of these individuals never met as they wrote on multiple continents at various periods of time, documenting several thousand years of divinely inspired revelation in three different languages—Hebrew, Aramaic, and Greek.

While this may make the Bible sound unmanageably complex, the truth is quite the opposite. Even though it consists of elements inherent to many different cultures, all the factors just mentioned work together to form one book that clearly illustrates what the *truly* ideal culture is. That culture is based on the relationship between a loving God and His creation. Let us build upon this premise and learn how this culture was established for all of humanity. Appropriately, we will begin with the book of beginnings—Genesis—and examine the material culture present during the founding of our world in *Genesis 1:1–5 (King James Version):*

> In the beginning God created the heaven and the earth. And the earth was without form, and void; and darkness was upon the face of the deep. And the Spirit of God moved upon the face of the waters. And God said, Let there be light: and there was light. And God saw the light, that it was good: and God divided the light from the darkness. And God called the light Day, and the darkness he called Night. And the evening and the morning were the first day.

These verses describe a point in time and space at which God— or in Hebrew, *Elohim,* which means "Creator"—formed the universe as we read in the words "the earth was without form, and void; and darkness was upon the face of the deep."

We are introduced to a culture of darkness. All the physical evidence of this culture indicates that the earth was without discernible shape. It was a completely empty space, immersed in water, devoid of any form of light, and filled with chaos.

This was a dismal culture but one with the potential for greatness as evidenced by the fact that "the Spirit of God moved upon the face of the waters." Let us take a moment to investigate this.

The Sevenfold Spirit of God

The Spirit of God is a sevenfold spirit. This is revealed in several verses including *Revelation 4:5:* "And out of the throne proceeded lightnings and thundering and voices: and there were seven lamps of fire burning before the throne, which are the seven Spirits of God."These seven spirits are specifically identified in *Isaiah 11:2:* "And the Spirit of the Lord shall rest upon Him, the Spirit of wisdom and understanding, the Spirit of counsel and might, the Spirit of knowledge and of the fear of the LORD." Seven, not coincidentally, is the number used in Scripture to represent divine perfection.

The specific spirit that served as the vessel through which the universe was created was the spirit of wisdom. This can be inferred from Proverbs 8:12, 22–30:

I, wisdom, dwell with prudence, and find out knowledge of witty inventions.

The Lord possessed Me in the beginning of His way, before His works of old. I was set up from everlasting, from the beginning, or ever the earth was. When there were no depths, I was brought forth; when there were no fountains abounding with water. Before the mountains were settled, before the hills was I brought forth: While as yet He had not made the earth, nor the fields, nor the highest part of the dust of the world. When He prepared the heavens, I was there: when He set a compass upon the face of the depth: When He established the clouds above: when He strengthened the fountains of the deep: When He gave to the sea His decree, that the waters should not pass His commandment: when He appointed the foundations of the earth: Then I was by Him, as one brought up with Him: and I was daily His delight, rejoicing always before Him.

If these verses sound familiar—if they perhaps make you think of the Lord Jesus Christ—there is good reason for this. We must remember that we serve a triune god, a god who exists as one being in three distinct persons. In fact, in Hebrew, *Elohim* is a plural word representing a single body collectively made up of multiple individuals. If this is confusing, a simple parallel may make the concept clearer. The church is also one body composed of many members and thus, the same description applies. Consider *1 John 5:7:* "For there are Three that bear record in heaven, the Father, the Word, and the Holy Ghost: and these Three are One." Consider *John 1:1–3, 14:*

In the beginning was the Word, and the Word was with God, and the Word was God. The same was in the beginning with God. All things were made by Him; and without Him was not anything made that was made.

And the Word was made flesh, and dwelt among us (and we beheld his glory, the glory as of the only begotten of the Father) full of grace and truth.

It is therefore not disrespectful to the Son of God for us to focus on the sevenfold Spirit of God here. Scripture makes perfectly clear that every person in the Trinity was at work during the creation of our universe. God the Father created all things through the power of the word of His son using the Spirit of wisdom as His vessel.

Light versus Darkness

Let us move our discussion to the topic of light for a moment, specifically those verses in which Scripture states that "God said, Let there be light: and there was light. And God saw the light, that it was good: and God divided the light from the darkness." What it is important for us to understand here is that these verses are not referencing the light of the sun but rather the light of God. Bearing this in mind, I would ask you to reflect upon *1 John 1:5:* "This then is the message which we have heard of Him, and declare unto you, that God is light, and in Him is no darkness at all." God is absolute in perfection and absolute in holiness. In Him, only goodness dwells, and from Him, only goodness emanates.

Remember that we are attempting to establish a foundation that will allow us to gain a better understanding of the ideal culture. Considering the combination of the verses related above, it is significant that this is where God begins to contrast the difference between light and darkness and between day and night. Prior to this point, everything was chaotic. When God began to illuminate creation with His presence, everything changed. What was once chaotic then had order and, by extension, became good. It is important that we take note here because by this action, God distinguished Himself from all other deities, as well as branded the culture of light with His own nature.

Let us not lose sight of the twofold spiritual message being presented. Not only are light and darkness being distinguished from one another but also good and evil as well as believer and nonbeliever. We see this concept throughout Scripture, as in 1 Thessalonians 5:5, "You are all the children of light, and the children of the day: we are not of the night, nor of darkness," as well as 2 Corinthians 6:14, "Be you not unequally yoked together with unbelievers: for what fellowship has righteousness with unrighteousness? And what communion has light with darkness?" As with the division of light and darkness, there is a spiritual division of cultures that has been made, and each of us must make a choice as to which culture we will belong. This is shown in 1 John 1:6–7: "If we say that we have fellowship with Him, and walk in darkness, we lie, and do not the truth: But if we walk in the light, as He is in the light, we have fellowship one with another, and the blood of Jesus Christ His Son cleanses us from all sin."

The point made here is simple and unassailable: We belong either to the light of God or the darkness of sin. It must be one or the other; we cannot belong to both.

The Firmament

The second aspect of the ideal culture is described in *Genesis 1:6–8:*

> And God said, let there be a firmament in the midst of the waters, and let it divide the waters from the waters. And God made the firmament, and divided the waters which were under the firmament from the waters which were above the firmament: and it was so. And God called the firmament Heaven. And the evening and the morning were the second day.

In this passage, the firmament describes the expanse of the sky separating the waters of the earth from the waters of the heavens. This is significant for multiple reasons. First, it introduces the conduit through which the water cycle has been made possible. The atmosphere is a storehouse for water, and the superhighway used to move it across the globe. Liquid water evaporates into vapor and ascends into clouds that are, in turn, carried across the world by winds. Cooler temperatures allow this vapor to condense into liquid once more, which then falls back to the earth as precipitation.

Much more importantly, these verses also provide details regarding the creation of the heavens.

> It is He that sits upon the circle of the earth, and the inhabitants thereof are as grasshoppers; that stretches out the heavens as a curtain, and spreads them out as a tent to dwell in. (Isaiah 40:22)

The "circle of the earth" upon which God is seated is the firmament of heaven, the Hebrew word for which—*shamayim*—is plural.

This brings up an interesting issue. According to Scripture, there were three levels of heaven created by God. The first of these is the *atmospheric heaven.* This is the sky or the *troposphere,* the region of breathable atmosphere that blankets the earth. This is the level of heaven cited in *Psalm 147:8:* "Who covers the heaven with clouds, who prepares rain for the earth, who makes grass to grow upon the mountains." Next is the *planetary heaven* where God has placed the stars, the moon, and the planets. In *Psalm 8:3–4*, it says, "When I consider Your heavens, the work of Your fingers, the moon and the stars, which you have ordained; What is man, that You are mindful of Him?" This is an obvious reference to the second level of heaven. David ponders the insignificance of mankind when compared to the greatness of God. Finally, there is the *third heaven,* commonly known as the dwelling place of God. It is this level of heaven that is mentioned in *2 Corinthians 12:2:* "I knew a man in Christ above fourteen years ago, (whether in the body, I cannot tell; or whether out of the body, I cannot tell: God knows; such a one caught up to the third heaven." It is also this level of heaven to which John refers in *Revelation 4:1–3:*

> After this I looked, and, behold, a door was opened in heaven: and the first voice which I heard was as it were of a trumpet talking with me; which said, Come up hither, and I will show you things which must be hereafter. And immediately I was in the spirit: and, behold, a throne was set in heaven, and One sat on the throne. And He that sat was to look upon like jasper and a sardine stone: and there was a rainbow round about the throne, in sight like unto an emerald.

There are many things we should draw from this information. First, it demonstrates that God has made provision for all things in the ideal culture He has created. Nothing happens by accident or chance but rather according to His very specific plan and design. Secondly, despite what could be viewed as mankind's seeming insignificance in the vastness of creation, the reality is that God has a very definite and unique purpose for each human being He has imbued with life. Also, and even more importantly, no matter where human beings may reside on this planet, because we serve a God who rules the heavens, we can be certain that we are never beyond His watchful eye. This should be a great comfort to redeemed believers, but also a great concern for those still enslaved by sin.

Scripture introduces a third example of collective evidence that constitutes God's ideal culture:

> And God said, Let the waters under the heaven be gathered together unto one place, and let the dry land appear: and it was so. And God called the dry land Earth; and the gathering together of the waters called He Seas: and Godsaw that it was good. And God said, Let the earth bring forth grass, the herb yielding seed, and the fruit tree yielding fruit after his kind, whose seed is in itself, upon the earth: and it was so. And the earth brought forth grass, and herb yielding seed after his kind, and the tree yielding fruit, whose seed was in itself, after his kind: and God saw that it was good. And the evening and the morning were the third day. (Genesis 1:9–13)

These verses illustrate God's creation not only of dryland and the waters that surround it but also the natural environments of every region the world over. To begin our discussion on this subject, I would first like to familiarize you with the Hebrew word for "Earth," *erets*—a term that can also be used to describe an entire created sphere or material realm. The Greek equivalent for this word is *gé*, which can be used to designate either the entire globe or an area of land distinguished by the context in which the word is used. This distinction is important because when reading or studying the Bible, many times, we find that there are cultures designated primarily by the region or country in which they dwelled. The Egyptians in the Old Testament are examples of this.

Historically speaking, God has dealt with only a specific people in a region while others have been spared. An example that confirms this truth can be found in *Exodus 10:21–23:*

> And the Lord said unto Moses, stretch out your hand toward heaven, that there may be darkness over the land of Egypt, even darkness which may be felt. And Moses stretched forth his hand toward heaven; and there was a thick darkness in

all the land of Egypt three days: They saw not one another, neither rose any from his place for three days: but all the children of Israel had light in their dwellings.

Though the Egyptians were punished, the Hebrews were spared. This is evidence that even in our fallen culture, God will not charge the sins of a single people to the entire world. In His ideal culture, sin will not exist at all.

The gathering of the waters and the creation of plants and other foliage to cover the land both demonstrate another means by which a loving God provided for the needs of His people. Human beings cannot live without water and sustenance. Although a large part of the earth was left as dryland, the Lord still formed the rivers and lakes that channel to the sea to meet the first of these needs. This, in turn, introduced the ecosystems—self-sustaining communities comprised of interdependent organisms—and established the food chain through which all creatures gain the nutrients essential to their survival. Once again, Scripture demonstrates that in God's ideal culture, full provision for the survival of His creation has been afforded.

CONCLUSION

To this point, we have discussed various aspects of God's ideal culture. To summarize, it is one in which the Lord reigns supreme over all His creation. It is a culture based on His design, based on order and wisdom. It is a pure and holy culture illuminated by the very presence of the Lord's perfection, a culture in which holiness and sin, good and evil, are understood to stand in stark contrast to one another. At no time and in no manner, they don't ever coexist, nor is there ever any "gray area" leaving any question as to what is right and what is wrong. It is also a culture in which there is no want because God has made abundant provision for every need of His created beings, beings that can never move beyond the scope of His loving care and attention, a culture blessed by God in every conceivable way.

The beauty of the ideal culture God has fashioned is that it is universal. It belongs to no single ethnic group, race, or region but rather to each one of God's creations. Sadly, we know that this culture was lost, and *Romans 5:19* reminds us how "...by one man's disobedience many were made sinners." Adam's failure in the garden of Eden allowed sin and death to enter the perfection of God's creation. Fortunately, that is not where the story ends for the same verse just cited concludes by saying "…by the obedience of One shall many be made righteous" although there will be hostility between the culture of light and the culture of darkness for as long as we walk the earth in these fleshly bodies. Our Father in heaven has provided a means by which the ideal culture will be redeemed, and mankind will once again enjoy the fullness of its wonder. This is evident in *John 3:16–17:*

> For God so loved the world, that He gave His only begotten Son, that whosoever believes in Him should not perish, but have everlasting life. For God sent not His Son into the world to condemn the world; but that the world through Him might be saved.

We must be careful here for this is not only one of the most often quoted verses in Scripture but also one of the most misinterpreted. These verses do not suggest that simply because the Lord Jesus Christ gave His life for us, all mankind is saved. Yes, the blood of Jesus was shed as a final sacrifice for sin. Yes, the blood of Jesus does indeed redeem us and free us from the chains by which sin binds us to the fallen world. Salvation does not come unless we first recognize that we are indeed sinners who are incapable of freeing ourselves from the bondage of sin. We must choose to embrace His sacrifice and, by extension, choose to enter this ideal culture once more.

According to John 14:6, the only path to salvation is through the Lord Jesus Christ: "Jesus said unto him, 'I am the Way, the Truth, and the Life: no man comes unto the Father, but by Me.'" His sacrifice was made as a promise to mankind, an investment in mankind's eternal future.

It is through His death on the cross, as God's perfect sacrifice for sin, and His resurrection three days later that we can now have eternal life in the ideal culture if we believe in Him.

My hope is that you will choose to enter the ideal culture of God through the redemptive work of the Lord Jesus Christ. If you have not done so, I urge you to allow the Spirit of God to work upon you that you may do so now. If you have, I encourage you to fight the good fight of faith to manifest the ideal culture to others.

Once again, until the next time. May the Lord bless and keep you all in His glorious light and love.

UNIT 2 DISCUSSION QUESTIONS

1. How would you describe the culture to which you belong?
2. What are some of the various elements that compose this culture? Specifically, what are some of the behaviors, beliefs, and values inherent to this culture?
3. How do you demonstrate these behaviors, beliefs, and values in your own life?
4. How would you describe the current culture of the world?
5. What are some of the high and low points of this culture?
6. How do you believe this culture compares to the ideal culture God has created?
7. In a secular sense, do you believe that various cultures can coexist peacefully?
8. If so, what are some of the benefits of such coexistence?
9. If not, what are some of the primary hindrances that can prevent a peaceful coexistence?
10. What about the coexistence of cultures in a spiritual sense?
11. Is it possible for us to belong to both the secular and spiritual cultures?
12. Why do you maintain the position that you do?
13. Why are social sciences so important?
14. What are your innate characteristics as compared to your experiences?
15. In your cultural subset, where do you identify yourself?
16. Does your culture relate more to the ideal or real culture and how?
17. Can the ideal culture truly be apprehended? Explain how.

UNIT 3

Who You Are—A Study of "Purpose"

Introduction

Welcome, brothers and sisters. Let us take this moment to thank God for all His many blessings. As always, it is a pleasure to join you as we once again delve into the spiritual truths that God has established in His Word. Before we get too involved in this undertaking, let us briefly review the information we have covered in our previous lessons in this series of *Do You Know What's Invested in You?*

We first investigated the concept of *self*. In that study, we examined the science of biology and thereby gained a scientific understanding of humanity's origin. We followed this by examining the Word of God and learned what it has to say about our strengths, abilities, gifts, and purpose. Finally, we introduced the four seeds of curiosity, faith, steadfastness, and patience, all of which the Lord has planted in us to spur various aspects of our human development.

We next investigated the concept of *culture*. We began by defining what this term means and how it affects our lives, as well as how it is passed from generation to generation. We also examined various social sciences and the theories of nature versus nurture, learning how both material and nonmaterial elements, as well as biological and environmental factors, influence and shape the development of a society's belief system. Finally, we discussed the difference between the ideal and real culture. As well, we examined the ideal culture outlined in Scripture.

Self and *culture* are two factors that can exert significant influence on a person's life. Today, we move on to the third and final factor considered in this series that influences our lives: *purpose.* This concept, hidden in the core of the other two, centers on the reason for which something is done, created, or exists.

How do you define purpose?

Purpose Defined

We are often lured into thinking that the purpose of life equates to establishing a career, gaining upward social mobility, accumulating wealth, and holding power. These things are neither wrong nor bad; they are however only a means to an end. Those who seek only these elements of life are ultimately left wanting; their lives are never truly fulfilled. The reason for this is simple. Humanity's purpose extends far beyond the self-centered, materialistic view so prevalent in society today. It extends even beyond our lifetimes in this world. The intention of this lesson is to highlight why and how this is true.

To assist us in accomplishing this, let us first delve a little more deeply into the worldly definition of purpose. Since the foundation upon which Western civilization was built began in ancient Greece, we will examine the positions of three of the greatest Grecian philosophers to gain insight into this topic.

Of the three ancient philosophers discussed in this lesson—Socrates, Plato, and Aristotle—which do you believe had the most accurate understanding of mankind's purpose?

Socrates

The first of these philosophers was Socrates, the son of a sculptor and a midwife. The focus of Socrates's public teaching rested on the extent of an individual's ability to acquire self-knowledge, which is the desire "to seek to know self." Socrates believed ignorance to be the enemy of understanding; this included ignorance of a person's faults, weaknesses, and negative tendencies. Socrates believed that only after a person recognized these things could he or she attain self-improvement and wisdom, both of which are lifelong pursuits.

Socrates further believed that goodness and truth, positive essences, and pure ethical and moral instincts were divinely placed in the soul. He contended, however, that these elements could not be brought to a level of conscious awareness unless they were first awakened or learned. According to his belief system, it is the destiny of mankind to seek out virtues such as courage, self-control, and propriety rather than ambitious or emotional desires that can cloud the quest for truth. When you think about this, I would like you to think about that teacher that you thought was hard on you or really didn't care. You will come to understand these virtues were something that teacher knew you would need to become the best version of yourself and to find and fulfill your purpose. The truth about self is the key success or failure in life. It was truth that Socrates loved and believed in. For Socrates, philosophy, which literally means "loving knowledge and wisdom," was a sacred path, a holy quest.

Plato

Plato is the second of the three philosophers we will discuss. Plato, whose actual name was Aristocles, was born into a wealthy and powerful family. He came under the influence of Socrates when he was approximately twenty years old and afterward decided to devote himself to the study of philosophy as well.

Plato viewed the world as being both idealistic and rationalistic. As such, he divided reality into two separate but related parts. On one hand, there was *phenomenon*—the material, temporal, and spatial manifestation of life; included in this were the appearance of things and the perceptions people have of them. On the other hand, there was ontos—the ideal or the ultimate reality, which is permanent, eternal, and spiritual. He believed phenomena are illusions that decay over time and ultimately die; ideals, by contrast, he maintained to be unchanging and perfect.

According to Plato, phenomena are available to a person through his or her senses and ontos through thought. Plato believed thought to be a vastly superior means of uncovering truth than its counterpart, the senses. A person's senses, he argued, can only provide information about the ever-changing and imperfect world of phenomena. Because of this, they can only provide a person with allusions to impressions of ultimate reality rather than ultimate reality itself. Thought, however, he believed could go straight to the core of the true self.

We just learned that the phenomenon is available to a person through his or her senses, and ontos the ideal or the ultimate reality, which is permanent, eternal, and spiritual. Plato suggested that there was a war going on between the phenomenal world, which strives to become ontos or the ideal or the ultimate reality. He applied this same dichotomy to human beings. He contended that the human body is material, mortal, and "moved," meaning that it is influenced by outside forces and circumstances. The soul, he believed, is part of the ideal, immortal, and unmoved. This is where we choose if we are going to allow our senses to govern our lives or we are going to transcend our senses and allow our spiritual to govern our lives. This is the true essence of the meaning to exercise and enjoy free will.

Plato identified the ideal with the gods and perfect goodness. The soul—composed of reason, self-awareness, and moral sense—he believed to be drawn to the good, the ideal, and, by extension, the divine. Plato's belief is that one's purpose in life is to closely resemble the divine, to draw nearer to the pure world of the ideal. For Plato, this constituted self-realization.

Aristotle

The third and final philosopher we will discuss is Aristotle. Aristotle was born in a small Greek colony called Stagira, located in Thrace. His father, a physician, taught him to take an interest in the details of natural life. As a result, Aristotle became as much a scientist as he was a philosopher. He was endlessly fascinated with nature and went a long way toward classifying the plants and animals of Greece. He was equally interested in studying the anatomies of animals and their behavior in the wild.

Just as Plato had been a student of Socrates, so was Aristotle a student of Plato. He was in fact Plato's prized student even though he disagreed with his teacher on many points. One issue on which the two experienced a difference of opinion was that of the phenomenal and the ideal. While Plato separated the ever-changing phenomenal world from the eternal ideal reality, Aristotle suggested that ideals could be found inside phenomena and that aspects of the universal were located inside the particulars of daily life.

What Plato called the ideal, Aristotle called essence; what Plato referred to as matter, Aristotle labeled as pure potential. Essence, to Aristotle, was perfect and complete but was without substance or solidity. He believed that essence made matter real and that it provided the shape, form, and purpose for material things. In his view, each was dependent upon the other to exist.

This process of moving from what was formless to possessing actual being he referred to as entelechy, a term which some translated as meaning "actualization." In Aristotle's philosophy, there were four causes that contributed to entelechy. First, there is the material cause, or the substances of which something is made. Second is the efficient cause, or the energy that changes matter. Third, there is the formal cause, or the shape, form, or essence that matter takes or by which it is defined, and the final cause, or its purpose or the reason for its existence.

How can you mesh the secular and the spiritual into your life?

Transition from Secular to Spiritual

This has been but a brief introduction to these philosophers and their theories, but it will be enough for our needs in this lesson, gaining a deeper understanding of mankind's purpose both now and in eternity. To do this, our understanding of purpose must be centered in the spiritual realm. We must come to better understand this concept from God's perspective rather than our own.

Through our investigation of God's Word, we will come to see that God revealed nuggets of truth even to these men.

What are some of those nuggets? Explain.

Hints of Scripture in the Philosophy of Socrates

As previously touched upon, Socrates made some interesting comments about mankind and its purpose. Three are worthy of note because of the scriptural tenets he unknowingly acknowledged through them. We will cover each of these in turn.

First, Socrates maintained that recognizing one's faults leads a person to wisdom. To overcome one's failings, he maintained that a person must first be able to recognize them. This belief harbors a very fundamental scriptural truth, one clearly expressed in *1 John 1:8–10:*

> If we say that we have no sin, we deceive ourselves, and the Truth is not in us. If we confess our sins, He is faithful and just to forgive us our sins, and to cleanse us from all unrighteousness. If we say that we have not sinned, we make Him a liar, and His Word is not in us.

If we ever hope to know God and to experience His truth, we must first recognize that we are sinners. Only once we confess this can a just god pardon us of our iniquity. This is only possible through the shed blood of Jesus Christ as Scripture tells us in *John 14:6:* "Jesus saith unto him; I am the way, the truth, and the life: no man cometh unto the Father, but by me."

The Son cannot be a part of our lives unless we first recognize that we are sinners. This applies to everyone as found in *Romans 3:23:* "For all have sinned, and come short of the glory of God."

Only by recognizing our own weakness can the Lord make us strong.

Socrates also mentioned that goodness must be awakened. A person cannot be either ethical or moral unless such concepts are first brought to life within them. Is this not the very point made by Apostle Paul in *Ephesians 5:8 and 13–14:*

> For you were sometimes darkness, but now are you light in the Lord: walk as children of light.
>
> But all things that are reproved are made manifest by the light: for whatsoever does make manifest is light. Wherefore He says, 'Awake you that sleep, and arise from the dead, and Christ shall give you light.'"

Though the perfect God has created us, we are born into unrighteousness through the sin of Adam. Only the righteousness of the Son of God can redeem us. This is clear in Romans 5:12–15:

> Wherefore, as by one man sin entered into the world, and death by sin; and so death passed upon all men, for that all have sinned: (For until the law sin was in the world: but sin is not imputed when there is no law. Nevertheless death reigned from Adam to Moses, even over them that had not sinned after the similitude of Adam's transgression, who is the figure of him that was to come. But not as the offence, so also is the free gift. For if through the offence of one many be dead, much more the grace of God, and the gift by grace, which is by one man, Jesus Christ, hath abounded unto many.

This passage teaches us that we are lost in sin and spiritually dead unto God, but through the gift of God, we can be made alive to God. This is evident in *1 Corinthians 15:45,* "And so it is written, The first man Adam was made a living soul; the last Adam was made a quickening spirit," and in *Ephesians 2:1,* "And you hath he quickened, who were dead in trespasses and sins."

Finally, Socrates pointed out that the purpose of mankind is to seek out virtue. Once again, this point is clearly made in Scripture and, in this instance, is made in almost exactly the same words in *2 Peter 1:3–7:*

> According as His divine power has given unto us all things that pertain unto life and godliness, through the knowledge of Him that has called us to glory and virtue: Whereby are given unto us exceeding great and precious promises: that by these you might be partakers of the divine nature, having escaped the corruption that is in the world through lust. And beside this, giving all diligence, add to your faith virtue; and to virtue knowledge; And to knowledge temperance; and to temperance patience; and to patience godliness; And to godliness brotherly kindness; and to brotherly kindness charity.

Through His Holy Spirit, the Lord has imbued us with the power to live holy lives unto Him. Doing so is proof of His Spirit within us, evidence of the manifestation of Christ's righteousness awakened within us. It is an expectation of the converted, not a choice to be made.

Hints of Scripture in the Philosophy of Plato

The Spirit of God also spoke through Plato—though without his awareness—just as He did through Socrates. As with Socrates, three of his previously mentioned beliefs demonstrate a very direct scriptural influence.

First, Plato divided the earth into two spheres—the temporary, material realm and the eternal, ideal realm. The Lord Jesus Christ Himself commented upon the duality of our human existence in *John 17:14:* "I have given them Your Word; and the world has hated them, because they are not of the world, even as I am not of the world.

The world that Jesus refers to here is, of course, the carnal world in which we currently dwell, a world full of sin that will one day pass away according to *1 John 2:17:* "And the world passeth away, and the lust thereof: but he that doeth the will of God abideth forever."

We must come to understand that we are different in Christ than we are in the world. This is clear in *1 Peter 2:11:* "Dearly beloved, I beseech you as strangers and pilgrims, abstain from fleshly lusts, which war against the soul."

Plato also made mention of his belief that thought, not emotion, leads to enlightenment. This, too, is reflected in Scripture. The heart is said to be the home of human emotion, but Scripture warns us not to follow it blindly. This is evident in *Matthew 15:19:* "For out of the heart proceed evil thoughts, murders, adulteries, fornications, thefts, false witness, blasphemies." Believers instead are urged to use reason as God Himself encouraged in the following:

> Come now, and let us reason together, saith the Lord: though your sins be as scarlet, they shall be as white as snow; though they be red like crimson, they shall be as wool. (Isaiah 1:18)

> And the brethren immediately sent away Paul and Silas by night unto Berea: who coming thither went into the synagogue of the Jews. These were more noble than those in Thessalonica, in that they received the word with all readiness of mind, and searched the scriptures daily, whether those things were so. (Acts 17:10–11)

Paul praised the Bereans, who did not blindly accept the Gospel message he shared but instead first tested his words against the truth of Scripture.

It is through reason that we, as believers, are to search Scripture, allowing the Spirit of God to guide us and reveal to us the truths God would have us understand, truths we are to accept as children with the faith our Heavenly Father has endowed us with. Thought, coupled with faith, brings us to greater wisdom.

Finally, Plato maintained that the purpose of mankind is to strive toward the ideal. This is very much a tenet of spiritual faith. Verse after verse in Scripture implores us to live holy lives that are pleasing to God. Perhaps none, however, do so as clearly or as passionately as those of *1 John 2:3–6:*

And hereby we do know that we know Him, if we keep His commandments. He that says, I know Him, and keeps not His commandments, is a liar, and the Truth is not in him. But whoso keeps His Word, in him verily is the love of God perfected: hereby know we that we are in Him. He that says he abides in Him ought himself also so to walk, even as He walked.

None of us will ever live the life of sinless perfection that our Lord Jesus lived. Nevertheless, the Word of God calls us to live as He did. This can only imply one thing—despite our shortcomings and daily failures, we are to strive each and every day to follow *Philippians 3:14:* "I press toward the mark for the prize of the high calling of God in Christ Jesus."

Hints of Scripture in the Philosophy of Aristotle

By this point, it should come as no surprise that the Holy Spirit revealed nuggets of scriptural truth to Aristotle as well. From the information previously covered in this lesson, two points must be highlighted.

Aristotle maintained that essence makes all things real. In our modern understanding, *essence* is generally defined as "the intrinsic nature or indispensable quality of something." What this means is that what is essential rests in the core of everything we see.

As Creator, God is the essence of all things. This is clear in *Romans 11:36,* "For of Him, and through Him, and to Him, are all things," and in *Luke 19:39–40,* "And some of the Pharisees from among the multitude said unto him, Master, rebuke thy disciples. And he answered and said unto them, I tell you that, if these should hold their peace, the stones would immediately cry out."

Even the stones proclaim the greatness of God and that God's very nature is so evident in creation that the world is without excuse regarding its failure to believe in Him. This is evident in *Romans 1:20:* "For the invisible things of him from the creation of the world are clearly seen, being understood by the things that are made, even his eternal power and Godhead; so that they are without excuse."

The Word of God repeatedly says that God is the author of all things. Not only is God the essence of all things currently in existence, He is also the essence of all things that ever were and ever will be. The triune God has made real everything that exists.

As discussed, Aristotle also outlined the process of entelechy and the four causes behind it. Each of these four causes has a very clear spiritual connection.

First, the *material cause* of mankind, or the substance from which we were made, is clearly identified in *Genesis 2:7a,* "And the Lord God formed man of the dust of the ground," and second, the *efficient cause,* or the energy by which mankind was created, is clearly identified in *Genesis 2:7b,* "and breathed into his nostrils the breath of life; and man became a living soul. Third, the *formal cause* is clearly identified in *Genesis 1:26a:* "And God said, 'Let us make man in our image, after our likeness.'" Mankind was made in an image that is very specifically identified as being God Himself.

This brings us to the *final cause,* the reason for mankind's existence and the focal point of this entire lesson. You may think that this will require a great deal of time to explain. After all, if we posed this question to one hundred people met in passing, it is highly likely that we would get nearly the exact same number of different answers. The reason for this is that many of these individuals would be secularly minded. They would seek to answer the question from a worldly perspective. From a spiritual standpoint, however, there is but one answer, which is found in *Isaiah 43:7:* "Even every one that is called by my name: for I have created him for my glory, I have formed him; yea, I have made him."

The purpose of mankind is to honor and glorify God.

How do we accomplish this?

Genesis 1:28 gives us a general example where it says, "And God blessed them, and God said unto them, Be fruitful, and multiply, and replenish the earth, and subdue it: and have dominion over the fish of the sea, and over the fowl of the air, and over every living thing that moveth upon the earth." There are, of course, many ways believers can glorify God. Scripture is full of examples, instructions, and commands designed to help followers of Christ do just that. So many, in fact, that in order to cover them with any degree of specificity, we would have to embark on an entirely new study. Fortunately, Scripture sums up the core of this practice in a simple admonition: "And whatsoever you do in word or deed, do all in the name of the Lord Jesus, giving thanks to God and the Father by Him" (Colossians 3:17).

Nothing in our lives is to be excluded from the Lord. All things we do are to be performed with Jesus Christ first and foremost in our minds as if our service was being performed directly unto Him.

Considering everything we have discussed to this point, what especially are we meant to take away and apply to our lives?

One lesson we should all take care to remember is that believers are meant to come together to live and serve God together. We were not created to live lives of loneliness. We have been born into a body of believers that spans the entire world. Each of us has millions of spiritual brothers and sisters we will one day be united with for all eternity. Though we may be apart from many of them now, that does not mean we cannot serve together in one spirit every day.

Another lesson is that no matter how overwhelming the presence and power of sin may seem in our world, we must not succumb to it. We must instead rely upon the teachings, guidance, and strength of the Lord to shine as His lights in the darkness. Where are we to find the means of doing this other than through the Word of God?

If we look at everything that has been created, we see the interconnectedness that makes us family. Just as execution of God's purpose would come through the first family in the beginning, so should its seeds be planted in our world today. Family is universal and comes in many forms. It is therefore vital that the elements and expectations of God's purpose be introduced here. Before we move to the final section of this lesson, let us briefly examine what these elements and expectations are.

Element one: social organization

The first of these is *social organization*. This is represented by the various parts of society and how they function with one another. When any group organized for a specific purpose becomes essential to social life or social order in the normal state of society, it becomes a part of the social organization.

As has been previously touched upon, we were never meant to be alone or to act in isolation. We are accountable to and for each other as demonstrated in *Genesis 4:9:* "And the Lord said unto Cain, Where is Abel thy brother? And he said, I know not: Am I my brother's keeper?" We are also expected to show generosity to one another as exemplified in *Hebrews 13:16:* "But to do good and to communicate forget not: for with such sacrifices God is well pleased."

We are likewise expected to always live in a manner pleasing to God. This is evident in Micah 6:6–8:

Wherewith shall I come before the Lord, and bow myself before the high God? Shall I come before Him with burnt offerings, with calves of a year old? Will the Lord be pleased with thousands of rams, or with ten thousands of rivers of oil? Shall I give my firstborn for my transgression, the fruit of my body for the sin of my soul? He has shown you, O man, what is good; and what does the Lord require of you, but to do justly, and to love mercy, and to walk humbly with thy God?

Most importantly, we must follow the instructions laid out in *1 John 4:20–21:*

If a man says, I love God, and hates his brother, he is a liar: for he that loves not his brother whom he has seen, how can he love God whom he has not seen? And this commandment have we from him, that he who loves God love his brother also.

Element two: customs and traditions

The second element is comprised of *customs and traditions,* or the way we are meant to set about doing things according to God's purpose. While some may fear that this section will comprise a long list of "dos" and "don'ts," in actuality, the guidelines are laid out quite directly in *Deuteronomy 5:32–33:*

You shall observe to do therefore as the Lord your God has commanded you: You shall not turn aside to the right hand or to the left. You shall walk in all the ways which the Lord your God has commanded you, that you may live, and that it may be well with you, and that you may prolong your days in the land which you shall possess.

We can, of course, learn what these commandments are only by reading the Bible. We must never lose sight of the fact of which 2 Timothy 3:16 reminds us: "All Scripture is given by inspiration of God and is profitable for doctrine, for reproof, for correction, for instruction in righteousness."

Element three: language

The third element is *language,* or system of communication, which is to serve as the cornerstone of God's purpose. When I speak to you about language, I am speaking about an ideal language for an ideal culture, which manifests God's purpose. It should come as no surprise, therefore, that such a language is established upon the Word of God and is to be utilized to glorify Him.

> This book of the Law shall not depart out of your mouth; but you shall meditate therein day and night, that you may observe to do according to all that is written therein: for then you shall make your way prosperous, and then you shall have good success. (Joshua 1:8)

> "As for me, this is My covenant with them," says the Lord; "My Spirit that is upon you, and My words which I have put in your mouth, shall not depart out of your mouth, nor out of the mouth of your seed, nor out of the mouth of your seed's seed," says the Lord, "from henceforth and forever." (Isaiah 59:21)

From these verses, we can clearly discern the Lord's admonition to study His Word and allow His spirit to guide us as we learn how and when to speak.

"Death and life are in the power of the tongue: and they that love it shall eat the fruit thereof" (Proverbs 18:21), and more importantly, even nonbelievers can be brought to recognize godly purpose as we glorify God through the words we speak.

This is evident in 1 Peter 2:12: "Having your conversation honest among the Gentiles: that, whereas they speak against you as evil64 doers, they may by your good works, which they shall behold, glorify God in the day of visitation." It is essential that we learn to do so according to His will.

Element four: religion

This leads us to the fourth element, *religion,* and the purpose for it, which is the relationship between human beings and the sovereign

God. Elohim, as mentioned in our last lesson, is the Creator and Ruler of the universe, one being in three distinct persons. The religion that honors Him is described in *James 1:27:* "Pure religion and undefiled before God and the Father is this, to visit the fatherless and widows in their affliction, and to keep himself unspotted from the world."

"To visit the fatherless and widows in their affliction" can be understood as meaning to go to see them, to look after them, and to be ready to aid them. Such a religion is one built upon a sincere faith in God that is demonstrated through actions of selfless benevolence toward His creations, most certainly those who are in need. To keep ourselves unspotted from the world, we must heed the words of *1 John 2:15–17:*

> Love not the world, neither the things that are in the world. If any man loves the world, the love of the Father is not in him. For all that is in the world, the lust of the flesh, and the lust of the eyes, and the pride of life, is not of the Father, but is of the world. And the world passes away, and the lust thereof: but he that does the will of God abides forever.

Element five: form of government

The reason for us to be careful where our allegiance lies is simple, and it forms a nice segue into the final element of God's purpose in this lesson—the *form of government* upon which the entire structure of this is built, a government that centers upon God. Despite the fact that many forms of government exist in our modern world, with many different men and women possessing many different— and often opposing—political points of view in positions of power, in our relationship with God, there is only one being who has been granted the authority to rule. This is evident in *Isaiah 9:6–7:*

> For unto us a Child is born, unto us a Son is given: and the government shall be upon His shoulder: and His name shall be called Wonderful, Counselor, The mighty God, The everlasting Father, and The Prince of Peace. Of the increase of His government and peace there shall be no end, upon the throne of David, and upon His kingdom, to order it, and to establish it with judgment and with justice from henceforth even forever. The zeal of the Lord of hosts will perform this.

These verses, of course, reference the Lord Jesus Christ. He is, has always been, and ever shall be the only true authority and, as such, the one we must serve before any other.

Bringing It All Together

My dear brothers and sisters, although this lesson has been lengthy, the end is now in sight. If I may ask you for just a few minutes more, you will then be free to reflect on everything that has been shared with you today.

Having all the information presented in the preceding lessons, how would you answer the following question: *Do you know what's invested in you?*

Over the course of this series of lessons, I have posed the same question to you several times: Do you know what's invested in you? It is time now that we finally address this issue and ensure that each of us fully understands the answer.

The God of all creation, eternal and perfect in every regard, has granted each one of us life. Even though every aspect of existence deserves His equal attention and concern, above all other created things, He has chosen to grant mankind the fullness of His love.

Not only did He create us in His own image, not only did He quicken our souls by breathing His own Holy Spirit into us, not only did He endow men with the wisdom and ability to transcribe His Word so it could be passed down from generation to generation, but in addition to all of these things, He also set us apart for redemption. Although it would have been perfectly just of God to condemn mankind because of the disobedience of Adam, God has instead showered His love upon us and created a path for us to be restored to righteousness. He did this, of course, through the birth and death of His own son. This is evident in Romans 5:8: "But God commended His love toward us, in that, while we were yet sinners, Christ Died for us."

My dear brothers and sisters, although we could not be more undeserving, the very love, life, and death of the Lord of lords and King of kings have been invested in each one of us and all solely through the grace and mercy of God. For what greater gift could we ask? For what more blessed charity could we ever hope or dream? Love beyond measure has been poured out upon us. It is incumbent upon us to never lose sight of this and to live the truth of this fact every day of our lives.

CONCLUSION

As we close, we must come full circle in the fact that this series has never focused on religion, denomination, or the prominence of a religious leader. It has focused on you, giving insight to the four seeds of curiosity, faith, steadfastness, and patience in the hope of leading you to what Apostle Paul called a mystery. This is clearly stated in *Colossians 1:26–27:* "Even the mystery which hath been hid from ages and from generations, but now is made manifest to his saints: To whom God would make known what is the riches of the glory of this mystery among the Gentiles; which is Christ in you, the hope of glory."

Now you know what's invested in you. This is your moment to embrace this journey and allow God to develop these seeds in you that you may be able to manifest the attributes of God in your life and live a life of example to the world in the hope of glorifying God and bringing others out of darkness to the light.

The Bible makes it abundantly clear that God created man and that He created him for His glory. Isaiah 43:7, as we read above, confirms this where it states, "Even every one that is called by my name: for I have created him for my glory, I have formed him; yea, I have made him."

This was exemplified in the person of Jesus in John 17:4: "I have glorified thee on the earth: I have finished the work which thou gavest me to do." Let us seek to speak these words to God at the end of our journey, called life, on earth.

May the light of God shine upon you and through you. May it bring a new concept of self-awareness, opening a new path before you that you may participate in His ideal culture and guiding you to the fulfillment of your purpose, both in this life and in everlasting life yet to come.

Perhaps you could share some examples of what you now realize is invested in you.

May God, now and forever, continue to bless you. Amen.

Unit 3 Discussion Questions

1. How do you define purpose?
2. Of the three ancient philosophers discussed in this lesson— Socrates, Plato, and Aristotle—which do you believe had the most accurate understanding of mankind's purpose?
3. How can you mesh the secular and the spiritual into your life?
4. What are some of those nuggets? Explain.
5. How do we accomplish this?
6. Considering everything we have discussed to this point, what especially are we meant to take away and apply to our lives?
7. Having read all the information presented in the preceding lessons, how would you answer the following question: *Do you know what's invested in you?*

Perhaps you could share some examples of *what you now realize is invested in you.*

Do *You* Know What's Invested in *You?*

WORKBOOK

CONTENTS

Topic

Who You Are—A Study of "Self"
SECULAR FRAMEWORK

Unveiling Your Unique Identity: A Journey of Self-Discovery
SPIRITUAL EXPOSITION

Unveiling Your Spiritual Potential: The Four Seeds of
TRANSFORMATION

Who You Are—A Study of "Culture"
CULTURE DEFINED

Exploring Culture: From Beliefs to God's Ideal Culture
Who You Are—A Study of "Purpose"
PURPOSE DEFINED

Discovering Your Divine Purpose

Who You Are—A Study Of "Self"

WORKBOOK

SECULAR FRAMEWORK

Secular Framework emphasizes the importance of self-discovery beyond one's familial and cultural roots. It suggests that understanding one's family history through genealogy is a valuable but limited aspect of self-identity. To gain a more comprehensive understanding of oneself and humanity, individuals should also explore biological factors and the commonalities that unite all human beings.

It also discusses the significance of science and spirituality working in harmony to provide a holistic view of human identity. It highlights the unity of humanity, irrespective of economic, gender, ethnic, or cultural differences. The central questions raised are: "In what ways are we similar, and in what ways are we different?"

It then delves into the structural organization of the human body, focusing on three levels: cells, tissues, and the nervous system. Cells have specific tasks to sustain life, and tissues consist of closely cooperating cells. The nervous system plays a crucial role in sensing and responding to the environment.

Furthermore, it explains how cells and tissues combine to form organs, such as the heart, lungs, and liver. The circulatory system is used as an example of how organs collaborate to perform specific functions. In total, there are eleven major organ systems in the human body, all of which are essential for sustaining life for all of humanity.

WORKSHEET: UNVEILING YOUR UNIQUE IDENTITY: A JOURNEY OF SELF-DISCOVERY

We will embark on a journey of self-discovery, delving into the fascinating world of biology and human commonalities. Get ready to uncover what makes you truly unique and gain a deeper understanding of your place in the world.

Create a family tree to understand your ancestry and heritage.

Reflect on how your family history has shaped your identity.

Unveiling Your Unique Identity: A Journey of Self-Discovery

This engaging workbook aims to help you embark on a meaningful journey of self- discovery, embracing both your individuality and your commonalities with others. Through activities, reflection, and exploration, you'll gain a deeper understanding of your identity and the beauty of the human experience.

Identity Reflection

- Reflect on your journey of self-discovery.
- Write a personal statement about your unique identity and what you've learned.

Journey Inside Your Body

- Learn about the organization of the human body into cells, tissues, organs, and organ systems.
- Identify specific functions of cells, tissues, and organs in your body.

Organ System Discovery

- Explore the eleven major organ systems in the human body.
- Understand the vital roles each system plays in sustaining life.

SPIRITUAL EXPOSITON

Spiritual Exposition emphasizes the spiritual significance of the human body, it draws parallels between the physical body's interconnectedness and the unity within the church as depicted in 1 Corinthians 12:12. It highlights the idea that all individuals, regardless of their background or status, are unique creations of God. This uniqueness forms a global spiritual family. This underscores the importance of spiritual context and connection, emphasizing that science alone cannot explain eternal matters.

It explores the components of the human being: body, soul, and spirit, explaining their roles and origins according to biblical scripture. It emphasizes the significance of spiritual awareness and understanding, linking it to our identity as creations of God.

This section introduces four seeds essential for spiritual growth: curiosity, faith, steadfastness, and patience. It discusses how these traits contribute to personal development and relationship with God. The text offers examples from the Bible, such as Job's resilience and faith.

In conclusion, it encourages readers to explore their spiritual potential and to embrace the teachings of Scripture, even if they challenge existing beliefs. It invites individuals to accept God's unconditional love and develop the mentioned seeds for personal growth.

WORKSHEET: UNVEILING YOUR SPIRITUAL POTENTIAL: THE FOUR SEEDS OF TRANSFORMATION

This workbook takes you on a transformative journey, exploring the concept of the spiritual body and how it relates to your life. Based on biblical teachings, this workbook helps you delve deep into the four essential seeds of curiosity, faith, steadfastness, and patience, guiding you toward self-discovery and spiritual growth.

After Understanding the concept and importance of spiritual growth set goals for your spiritual journey

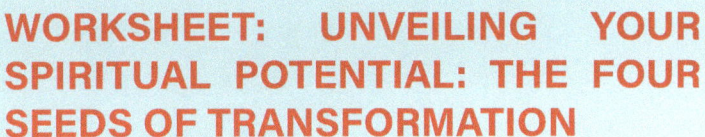

Curiosity - Seed 1

Exploring the power of curiosity in your spiritual journey by reflecting on biblical examples of curiosity

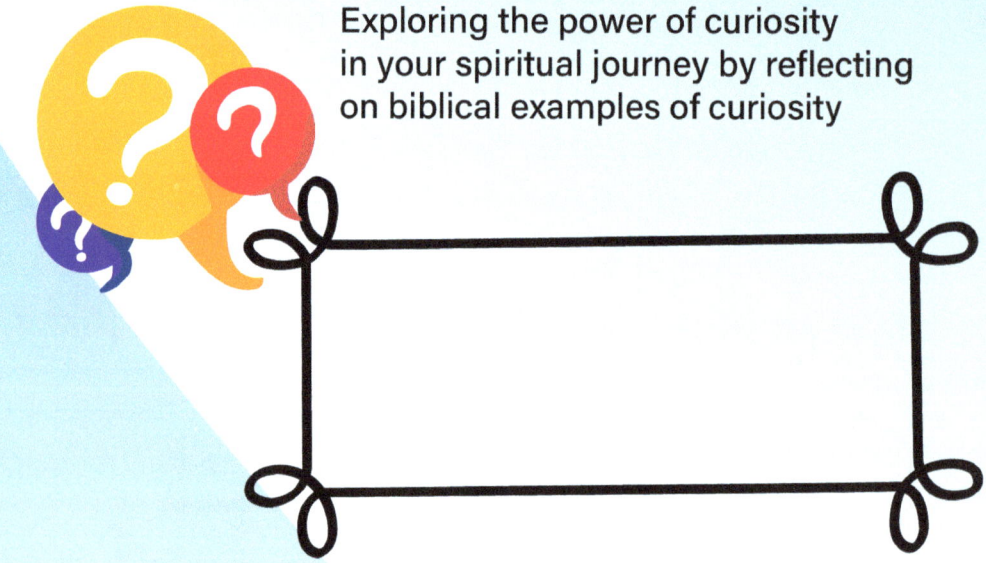

Exercises to awaken your spiritual curiosity.

1. Journaling: Start a spiritual journal where you record your thoughts, questions, and experiences related to your spirituality. Write about your beliefs, doubts, and the things that inspire you. Reflect on your spiritual journey.
2. Meditation and Mindfulness: Practice meditation and mindfulness to quiet your mind and become more in tune with your inner self. Consider exploring different meditation techniques from various traditions, such as Buddhist mindfulness or Christian contemplative prayer.
3. Nature Walks: Spend time in nature and connect with the natural world. Observe the beauty and complexity of creation. Many people find a deep sense of spirituality in nature.
4. Interfaith Dialogue: Engage in conversations with people from different faith backgrounds. Attend interfaith events or discussion groups to learn about their beliefs and practices. This can broaden your perspective and deepen your understanding of spirituality.
5. Artistic Expression: Use creative outlets like art, music, or writing to explore and express your spiritual thoughts and feelings. Creating art can be a deeply spiritual practice.
6. Spiritual Retreats: Consider attending a spiritual retreat or workshop to immerse yourself in a focused exploration of your faith or spirituality. Retreats often provide guidance and a supportive environment for introspection.
7. Questioning and Self-Reflection: Continuously ask questions about your beliefs and spirituality. Challenge your assumptions and seek answers to your spiritual inquiries through introspection and research.
8. Study Comparative Religion: Take a course or read books on comparative religion to gain a deeper understanding of the world's various faiths and their similarities and differences.

Faith - Seed 2

Differentiate between natural and spiritual faith and nurture your spiritual faith.

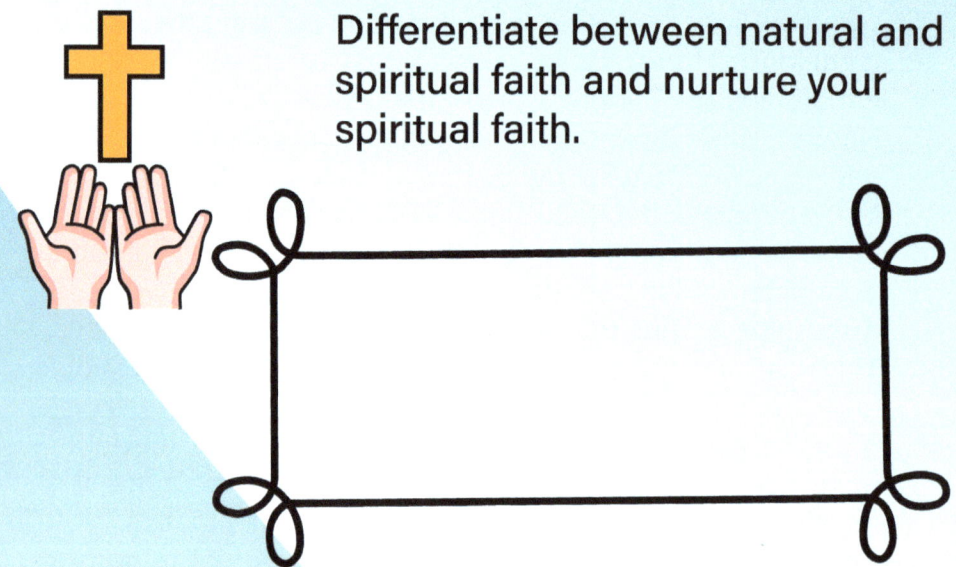

Scripture-based exercises to strengthen your faith.

1. Daily Scripture Reading:
    - Commit to reading a portion of the Bible every day. You can start with a specific book, such as the Psalms,
    - Journal your reflections and insights as you read. Record verses that resonate with you or prompt questions.
2. Memorization:
    - Choose key Bible verses or passages that are meaningful to you and commit them to memory. This can be a verse that encourages you, provides guidance, or speaks to your current situation.
    - Review and recite these verses regularly to keep them fresh in your mind and heart.
3. Meditation:
    - Practice biblical meditation by reflecting deeply on a passage or verse. Focus on its meaning and how it applies to your life.
    - Meditate on verses like Psalm 1:2, which says, "But his delight is in the law of the Lord, and on his law, he meditates day and night."
4. Fasting:
    - Consider incorporating fasting into your spiritual routine, seeking guidance from Scripture. Fasting can help you draw closer to God and develop self-discipline.
    - Follow the example of Jesus in Matthew 4:2, who fasted for 40 days and nights in the wilderness.
5. Acts of Service:
    - Put your faith into action by engaging in acts of service and charity. Matthew 25:35-36 highlights the importance of caring for others in need.
    - Seek opportunities to live out the teachings of Jesus through love and compassion.
6. Gratitude Journaling:
    - Keep a gratitude journal where you regularly write down things, you're thankful for. Reflect on God's blessings and faithfulness in your life.

Steadfastness - Seed 3

Understanding the role of steadfastness in your spititual life.

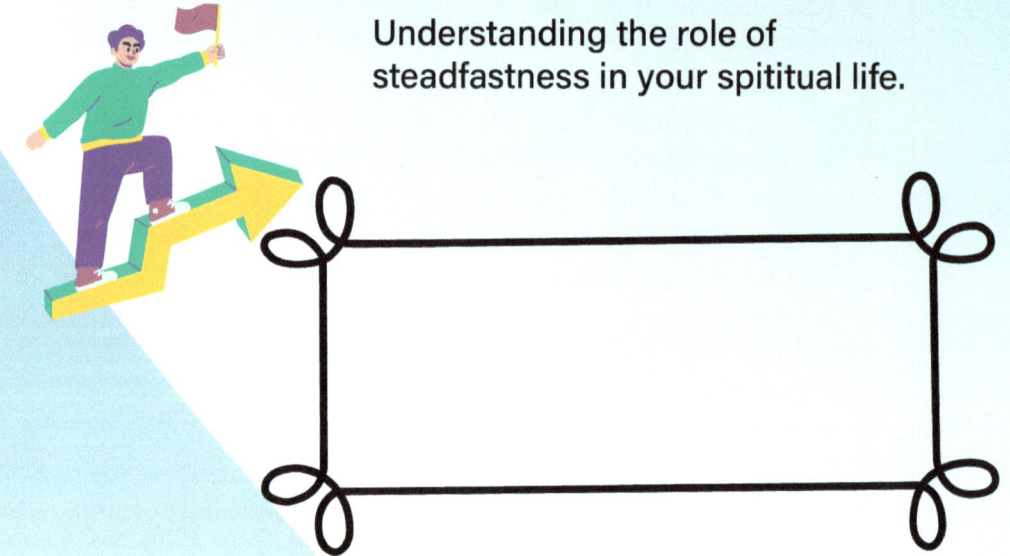

Practical exercises to develop steadfastness.

1. Set Clear Goals:
    - Identify specific, achievable goals in different areas of your life, such as personal growth, career, health, or relationships.
    - Break down larger goals into smaller, manageable steps to make progress more tangible.
2. Daily Habit Formation:
    - Establish positive habits that align with your goals. Consistency in daily routines can build discipline and resilience.
    - Start small and gradually increase the complexity of your habits over time.
3. Mindfulness Meditation:
    - Practice mindfulness meditation to enhance your ability to stay present and focused. It can help you better manage stress and maintain a calm, centered mindset.
4. Physical Exercise:
    - Regular physical activity boosts both mental and physical resilience. It can increase your endurance and reduce stress.
    - Engage in exercises you enjoy making it a sustainable part of your routine.
5. Learn from Setbacks:
    - Embrace failure and setbacks as opportunities for growth. Analyze what went wrong and how you can improve for the future.
    - Maintain a positive attitude and avoid dwelling on past mistakes.
6. Positive Self-Talk:
    - Cultivate a positive inner dialogue. Replace self-doubt and negativity with affirmations and encouraging self-talk.
    - Remind yourself of your capabilities and past achievements.
7. Practice Gratitude:
    - Regularly express gratitude for the positive aspects of your life. It can shift your perspective and help you stay motivated.

Patience - Seed 4

Discover the significance of
patience in spiritual growth.

Exercises to cultivate patience in your life.

1. Mindfulness Meditation:
    - Mindfulness meditation involves focusing your attention on the present moment without judgment. Regular meditation practice can increase your awareness of impatience triggers and help you respond more calmly
    - Start with short sessions and gradually increase the duration. Observe your thoughts and emotions without reacting to them and bring your attention back to your breath or a chosen focal point.
2. Slow Down:
    - Practice doing everyday tasks intentionally and at a slower pace. This can include eating, walking, or even driving more slowly.S
    - lowing down allows you to savor experiences, be more present, and reduce the rush that often leads to impatience.
3. Count to Ten:
    - When you feel impatience rising, take a deep breath and count to ten before reacting. This brief pause can give you the space to collect your thoughts and respond more thoughtfully.
    - If necessary, count to twenty or more to extend the time you must reflect before reacting.
4. Practice Active Listening:
    - Improve your patience in conversations by practicing active listening. Give the speaker your full attention without interrupting or formulating your response in your mind.
    - Ask clarifying questions and seek to understand the speaker's perspective before expressing your own.
5. Engage in Waiting:
    - Deliberately put yourself in situations where you must wait, such as standing in line or sitting in traffic. Instead of viewing this time as a nuisance, use it as an opportunity to practice patience.
    - Bring a book, listen to calming music, or simply observe your surroundings. Embrace waiting as a chance to be still and present.

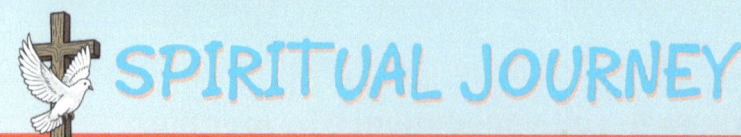

Unveiling Your Spiritual Potential: The Four Seeds of Transformation

- Summarizing the key lessons from each seed.
- Reflecting on your spiritual journey and set future goals for your spiritual growth.

_____

_____

_____

_____

_____

_____

_____

_____

Who You Are—A Study Of "Culture"

WORKBOOK

SPIRITUAL EXPOSITON

Culture encompasses the beliefs, behaviors, and characteristics shared by a group or society, including language, religion, cuisine, and more. It's closely tied to identity and a sense of belonging. Social sciences like archaeology, anthropology, and sociology help study and understand culture.

The nature versus nurture theory explores the influence of innate characteristics and experiences on an individual's development. Cultural subsets exist within larger cultures, and multiculturalism promotes diverse cultural coexistence.

Ideal culture differs from real culture, representing perfect values and norms compared to what people practice. The Bible's creation account emphasizes the importance of light, the firmament, and the earth, highlighting God's provision for creation's needs and the division between good and evil in God's ideal culture.

WORKSHEET: EXPLORING CULTURE: FROM BELIEFS TO GOD'S IDEAL CULTURE

This structured workbook will engage readers by providing a clear progression of concepts, encouraging reflection, and offering practical activities to enhance their understanding of culture and its various dimensions.

- **Explain the concept of culture and its various components. Provide real-life examples of cultural elements and your own cultural backgrounds and beliefs.**

The Three Social Sciences

Nurture vs. Nature

Delve into the nature vs. nurture theory.Discuss the role of innate characteristics and life experiences in shaping individuals.

Highlight the significance of each field in understanding culture.

Can you think of situations where nature and nurture interacted to shape a specific aspect of your development? How did these two factors work together or against each other?

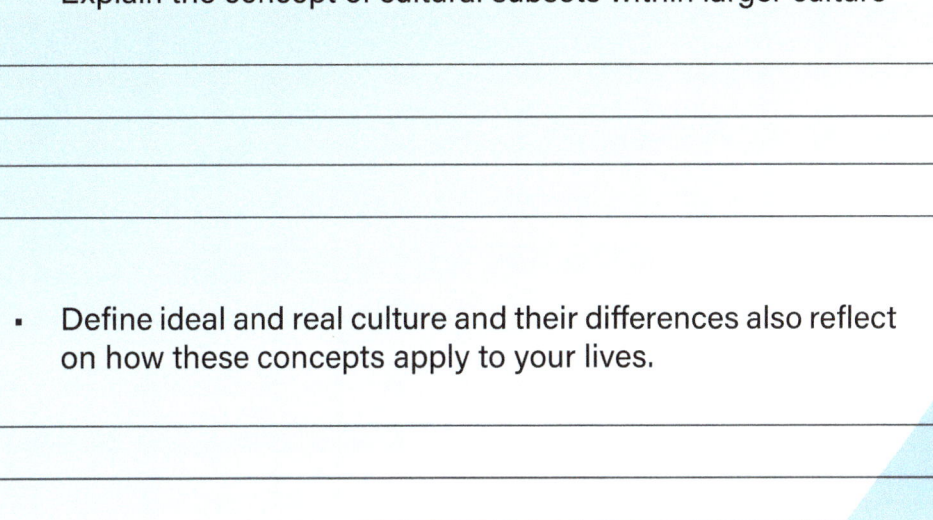

- Explain the concept of cultural subsets within larger culture

_____
_____
_____
_____

- Define ideal and real culture and their differences also reflect on how these concepts apply to your lives.

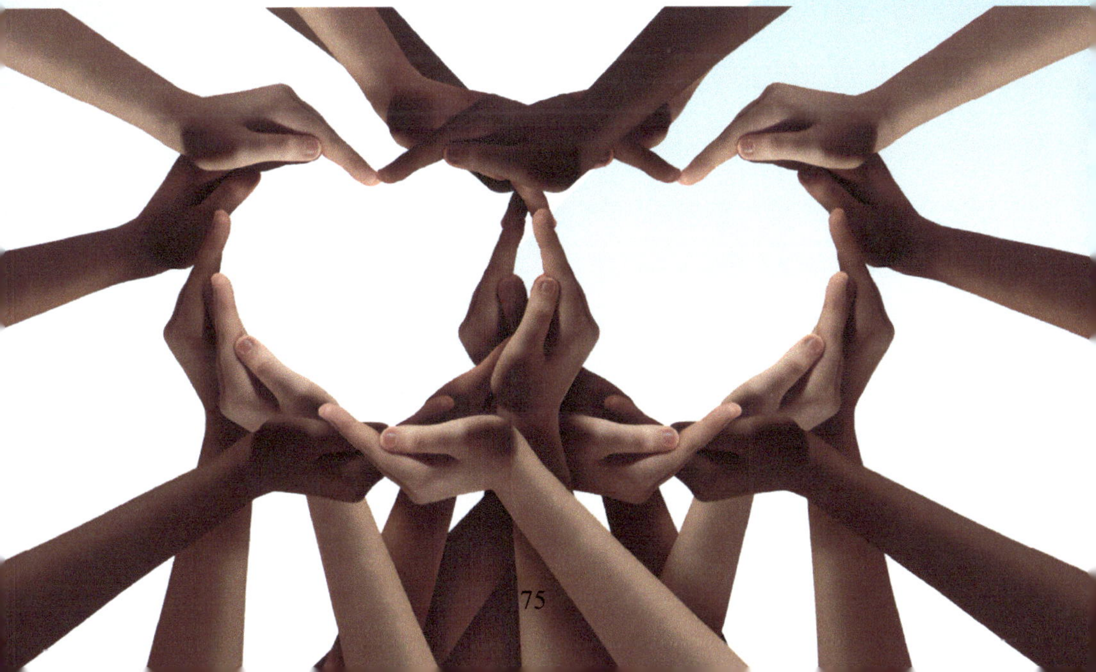

_____
_____
_____
_____

75

GOD'S IDEAL CULTURE

- Introduce the biblical perspective on culture and creation.
- Discuss the importance of light, goodness, and God's provision in ideal culture.

What specific actions or changes in your daily life do you believe would bring you closer to living in accordance with God's ideal culture? How can you implement these changes, and what support or resources might you need to do so?

Consider a recent situation where you faced a moral or ethical decision. Reflect on whether your choice aligned with what you perceive as God's ideal culture. If not, what alternative actions or decisions could have better reflected your values and beliefs? How can you apply these insights to future decisions and actions in your life?

_____

_____

_____

_____

_____

_____

_____

_____

Who You Are—A Study Of "Purpose"

WORKBOOK

PURPOSE DEFINED

This section discusses the purpose of life and explores the perspectives of three ancient Greek philosophers: Socrates, Plato, and Aristotle.

This section emphasizes that life's purpose extends beyond materialistic pursuits and self-centered goals. Socrates believed in self-knowledge and self- improvement, while Plato saw the world as divided into the material and ideal realms, emphasizing the pursuit of the ideal. Aristotle focused on essence, causes, and the purpose of existence.

This section also highlights the importance of recognizing faults, awakening goodness, and seeking virtue in one's life. They draw parallels between the philosophers' teachings and biblical scripture, emphasizing the need to recognize sin, awaken to righteousness, and seek virtue. The ultimate purpose of humanity, according to the author, is to honor and glorify God through living in accordance with His teachings and commands.

This section concludes by discussing elements that play a role in fulfilling God's purpose, including social organization, customs, language, religion, and a government centered on God. The author emphasizes the importance of living in a way that aligns with God's purpose and shows love and mercy to others.

Overall, this section explores the deeper meaning of life's purpose, drawing on philosophical perspectives and Biblical teachings to encourage readers to live a life that honors God and serves others.

WORKSHEET: DISCOVERING YOUR DIVINE PURPOSE

In this workbook, we will explore the concept of purpose from both philosophical and spiritual perspectives. We will delve into the teachings of ancient Greek philosophers such as Socrates, Plato, and Aristotle to gain insights into the meaning of life. Additionally, we will connect these philosophical ideas with biblical truths to help you discover your own purpose.

- **Briefly summarize each philosopher's (Socrates, Plato, Aristotle) views on purpose.**
- **Reflect which philosopher's perspective resonates most with yours.**

Platonic Ideals
vs.
Phenomenal Exercise

List of examples in your life that
represents the "phenomenal"
(temporary) and the "ideal" (eternal).
Reflect on howfocusing the ideal
can bring more purpose
and fulfillment to your life.

ARISTOTELIAN CAUSE IN YOUR LIFE
Identify one personal goal or aspiration and break it down using
Aristotle's four causes (material, efficient, formal, and final). How can
understanding these causes help you achieve your goal?

Reflecting on Personal Purpose

The Role of Faith

- Explore the role of faith in understanding and fulfilling one's purpose.
- Also share a personal story of how your faith has guided you in life.

- Think deeply about your own purpose in life.
- What are your passions and talents?
- How can you use them to serve others and honor God?

Write a concise statement that defines your life's purpose based on the insights gained from the book. Share this statement with a partner or group for feedback.

DAILY PRACTICES FOR PURPOSE

Practical daily practices can be instrumental in helping align with your purpose and live more intentionally.

Meditation and Mindfulness:
Practice meditation or mindfulness exercises daily to enhance self-awareness and focus.

Acts of Kindness:
Commit to performing one act of kindness each day, whether big or small, to contribute positively to others' lives.

Prayer of Reflective Journaling:
Set aside time for prayer, reflection, or journaling to connect with your inner self and explore values and aspiritions.

Gratitude Practice:
Cultivatea daily gratitude practice by reflecting on and appreciating the positive aspects of your life.

Community Engagement:
Dedicate time to engage with your community through volunteering, supporting local causes, or building meaning connections.

Setting Intentions:
Begin each day by setting clear intentions for how you want to live that day in alignment with your purpose.

CONSIDER THESE PRACTICES AND CHOOSE ONE THAT RESONATES WITH YOU THE MOST.

Create a daily plan that aligns with your purpose statement. Include specific actions, behaviors, or habits that will help you live a more purposeful life.

ABOUT THE AUTHOR

William Evans is the founder and pastor of the Church of Unity in Christ established February 2000. William comes from a God-fearing family that gave him a foundation of love, reverence, and faith in God. This led to him committing his life to the Lord Jesus Christ in 1987 under the guidance and leadership of the late Bro. McKinley Matthews of the House of the Lord located in Houma, Louisiana. There he learned the discipline needed to study and apply the Word of God. After five years being led by the Holy Spirit, William moved to Dallas, preaching and teaching in many churches, street ministries, nursing homes, etc. Finally settling in the church of New Hope under the tutelage of the late Pastor Sammy Thompson, there in 1999, he was licensed and ordained to preach the Word of God. Pastor Evans made a vow to God if God would teach him, he would teach his people. He has maintained that commitment throughout his ministry. The mantle that rests on Pastor Evans is to cause individuals to experience the glory of God like he did through the teaching, preaching, and application of the Word of God.

www.ingramcontent.com/pod-product-compliance
Lightning Source LLC
Chambersburg PA
CBHW040847120626
46547CB00001B/61